NO WAY OUT BUT THROUGH

NO WAY OUT BUT THROUGH

One Man's Journey from Mental Illness to Clarity and Strength of Soul

GRAHAM AITCHISON

CREATION
HOUSE

Library of Congress Cataloging-in-Publication Data:
2013930812
International Standard Book Number: 978-1-62136-348-4
E-book International Standard Book Number:
978-1-62136-349-1

While the author has made every effort to provide accurate telephone numbers and Internet addresses at the time of publication, neither the publisher nor the author assumes any responsibility for errors or for changes that occur after publication.

First edition

13 14 15 16 17 — 987654321
Printed in the United States of America

PROLOGUE AND DEDICATION

THIS BOOK IS a diary of the things I have learned about life, the world around me, and myself over the years and was written at the prompting of the Holy Spirit. It is not intended to judge anyone and is purely a reflection and interpretation of my own experiences.

The purpose of writing this book is to hopefully pass on some insight to any readers out there who may be able to gain something out of this book to help themselves in their own lives.

I would like to dedicate this book to God, without whom I do not believe I would be alive to tell this story; to my mother, Kaye, for her prayers, love, and kindness toward me over the years, as well as being a living example of how people's lives can truly change for the better through God; and my friend Dennis McCaskill, who runs Equip and Release Ministries in Hamilton, New Zealand, without whom this book would never have happened.

CONTENTS

INTRODUCTION

Beginnings

I WAS BORN IN Wellington, New Zealand, in January of 1984 as an only child to a two-parent household. On the outside, to those looking in, my childhood was relatively normal; however, internally it was a different story. From a young age I became strongly aware of a powerful sense of fear and uncertainty, as well as unwanted and intrusive thoughts. I had no idea what these were, and I found myself trying to manage what felt like an overpowering internal chaos within me that had no boundaries or limits. I found myself obsessively counting things around me, and my moods were highly unpredictable. It would have been easy to pass this off as simply being a moody child; however, I had a sense, even back then, that there was something more to it than simply adolescent mood swings.

I struggled with addictive behavior and terrible mood swings throughout my childhood and teenage years. My schoolwork suffered and my physical health was often in very poor shape. My relationships suffered due to the outworking of what I held within myself, which I had no idea how to manage or change at the time. This caused me to harbor a lot of anger and bitterness in my life. I felt misunderstood, misinterpreted, and unjustly treated, which made my attitude worse and caused people to treat me accordingly, which made my attitude worse again. It was a vicious cycle that I couldn't see any way of breaking.

Although I initially accepted Christ at a young age and had an awareness of God over the years, I did not fully dedicate myself to the Christian walk until shortly after my eighteenth birthday. I thought that this was going to automatically make everything OK and that I would now automatically be at peace; however, things for me only seemed to get worse, and my mental health seemed to only deteriorate further.

Upon a visit to a general practitioner I was diagnosed with a condition known as obsessive-compulsive disorder (or OCD), which is basically a mental disorder based around doubt. It manifests through the sufferer trying desperately to control everything around them in order to control the chaos they feel inside, but this does not solve anything. The sufferer feels that they have no choice but to obey the thoughts that they are bombarded with on a daily basis. I was also diagnosed with clinical depression and advised to start taking anti-depressant medication. I was prescribed the second highest recommended dosage of the medication that I was on, which was three capsules per day, and was basically told that I would be dependent on the medication for the rest of my life, that there was no cure for me, and the best I could hope to do was manage what was happening to me.

However, I felt very strongly that God did not agree with this prospect. I felt that He wanted to journey with me through everything that I carried within me and that healing and peace were available to me. It was going to be a hard journey with a lot of misunderstanding and confusion, but it was the only true path to the only real thing I have ever wanted in my entire life: peace.

I powerfully resisted the journey at first. I subconsciously knew what my own heart was like, and the last thing I ever wanted to do was take a hard look at myself, as I knew I would not like what I would find. However, I eventually began to see reason, that this was the only way to the kind of peace I truly desired in my life. It has been a very hard and painful journey, and there were times when I literally felt as if I were scouring my way through the depths of hell itself. I wanted to give up on the journey many times and would occasionally spend months—sometimes even years—stuck at the foot of an obstacle I simply did not know how to get past yet with nowhere else to go but forward. However, the Spirit of God continued to guide me, and I eventually began to realize that the peace I so desperately wished for was slowly being built into my life, piece by piece.

This book is the story of my journey, and I have attempted to divide it into three parts, the first part being about how I used to be before I became a Christian and before I began to learn how to change. The detail described in here has come out of hindsight. Only now, through all the lessons I have learned, have I been able to look back and accurately identify what was happening to me before I became a Christian. The second part describes how I began to learn to heal through the situations that God put me into and the various techniques and tools that He provided me with to help me break through what was holding me back. The third describes some of the lessons about life, theories I have developed, and observations I have made of the world around me, which I have gained over the experience of the years.

Part One

THE WAY THINGS WERE

ADDICTION

O NE OF MY biggest journeys throughout the years has been through addiction. I have one of those personalities that people would call an "addictive personality." The OCD traits in my life have certainly amplified this, and it has been one of my biggest struggles over the years.

Addiction for me was never as blatantly obvious as alcoholism or drug addiction; it was more subtle, and it came out in other ways. My strongest addiction was always toward people and relationships, which mainly became apparent throughout my teenage years. The dark, emotional core in my life (which at that point was not known to me) needed an outlet, and subconsciously I needed a release from the darkness, fear, and uncertainty that dwelled within me. Time and time again throughout my childhood and teenage years I would meet someone—they might be a friend, parental figure, or girlfriend—and I would connect with them. Although they did not realize it, they would trigger the emotional darkness and pain in me that needed to be medicated through acceptance. My subconscious mind would tell me, "*This person can heal you and make you whole. This person can complete you and fix everything.*" This was, of course, based in a lie. However, due to my lack of self-knowledge and understanding I allowed this to drive me forward into an obsessive relationship without even realizing it.

I had always felt as if my world had been shattered from the moment I was born. This was due to my failing mental health, which I was subconsciously aware of even at a young age. This need in me to have a safe and stable environment that could take anything thrown at it would cause me to latch on to people obsessively. They would become my entire world; everything they said or did would affect me. Even a word spoken that my mind could somehow conceive may be threat to me would cause my stomach to tie itself in knots through fear. I put myself in a dangerous position without even realizing it and threw myself into a vicious cycle guaranteed only to ever end in defeat. I would cling to them so tightly and would look to them for constant reassurance from something that I carried within myself. I ultimately looked toward them to fix my problems for me.

What I did not know was that the only way I could be free of this was not to obsess over them but to look in the mirror and face what was inside me. That was the real cause of my problem and the only way it could be fixed. However, I did not know this at the time, so I just continued to obsess, and life was OK just so long as I had that constant reassurance from that other person. Little did I know the destruction I was setting myself up for.

People began to tire of my obsessive behavior and began to pull away from me. Somewhere in my unstable mind I was forced to face what ultimately I already knew but never wanted to admit to myself: that people would let me down and could not be depended upon fully. However, although I had this knowledge within me, I was unable to face up to it and acknowledge it, even though the darkest part of my subconscious mind knew it to be true. This also began to translate into my relationships and made me even more obsessive.

This is where the cycle really began; I would cling to people out of expectation and then desperation. All the time I did this I was also subconsciously aware that despite how much I clung to them, they ultimately could not help me and would let me down even harder than before. It wasn't their fault; it was my unrealistic expectations of people. So, instead of them helping me to change my ways, it caused me to cling even tighter to them, which in turn magnified the fear to an even more powerful level, which caused me to cling tighter again. It was a vicious cycle, spiraling downward very rapidly. My self-destruction was inevitable. Eventually I would just continue to wear people out, and they would leave me, so I really became my own worst enemy. I was causing my greatest fears to come to life by acting out of them rather than trying to work through them.

This addiction in my life caused me to latch on to anything I thought could fix, and it would drive everything from my subconscious mind, where I was not aware of it. Relationships tended to be one of the main things I would grasp on to, but it would also give rise to other things I pursued with the same addictive tendencies, such as cigarette smoking. I would live my life trying to bury a part of me that I wanted to hide from. The most dangerous thing about OCD and most anxiety disorders in general is that they crave a resolution. However, the resolution is only ever temporary, though the sufferer is driven to search after that resolution at all costs, even if they know within themselves that the resolution ultimately will not satisfy them. It will just be a matter of time until the cravings for a solution resurface, and so the sufferer spends his or her entire existence chasing after a dream that can never be realized and chasing a goal that will never be met. Without enlightenment from the Holy Spirit and through their own honesty with themselves in the mirror, they will never be able to get out of it and will continue chasing something that will never be reached.

OBSESSIVE-COMPULSIVE DISORDER

Throughout my entire life I struggled with OCD; however, I was not officially diagnosed with it until I was twenty years old. I had always struggled with a strong sense of uncertainty and doubt and would often engage in obsessive behavior, often without even realizing it. I struggled to do anything with a sense of confidence and self-belief, as OCD is very strongly based on doubt. The way my thought processes would work usually involved an unwanted fear or doubt that thrust itself into my mind, and rather than being silenced by a sense of certainty and confidence I carried within, the fearful thought that entered my mind would trigger the fearful and negative emotions. So, without any sense of self-reassurance I would immediately seek some kind of external solution to the internal problem I was facing.

For example, when I walked up to the bus stop to take the bus to work in the morning, I would often become gripped with a powerful fear that I had left the door open, and I had an almost overwhelming urge to run back down to the house to check to see if the door was locked. I could try with my own strength to resist it, but the urge to run back down and check the door—in order to silence the internal torment I felt—was so powerful I very often gave in to it. Of course, it often made me miss the bus altogether and end up late for work! Most of the time, once I got back down to the house I would find that the door had been locked all along, and my fears that I had left it open were irrational and not based in reality. But, because I was not 100 percent certain at the time, I was unable to just push these fears away and continue up to the bus stop. This is just one example of the things I would do in order to try and control the chaos I was feeling inside.

Security was a big one. I was paranoid about my possessions being stolen. If I got something new that I treasured, my paranoia would go through the roof. I would continually check on things that I was worried about throughout the day out of fear that they may have been stolen, and if I was not able to check them I would worry about them incessantly until I had the opportunity to reassure myself.

I could take something that had happened or something that someone had said completely out of context and invent my own paranoid story about it in my own mind, which my fears would immediately pounce on. I would partake in other obsessive activities without realizing it, such as counting telephone poles while in the car with my parents, walking through a doorway several times over until it "felt right," and strongly avoiding small objects out of an irrational fear that I might swallow them. My mind was almost never at rest. I would often remain awake for hours throughout the night with my mind churning over fear-based thoughts and paranoia.

Other times, the fears in my life were cemented in my mind through circumstances. For example, once I didn't check the door properly while I was rushing out to work and came home to realize that I had left the door ajar all day with no one else home. Anyone could have walked in and stolen from our house. Incidents like these further fueled the fear-based control in my life and gave me even more reasons why I had to control things thoroughly. I felt that the moment I let my guard down, things like this would happen. The fear in my life, coupled with

myself, even positive com-
d not be properly received.
uld come whenever I felt I
was placed before me—or
something terribly wrong—
ould send me into a black
ared greatly. To keep myself
uld do everything that I pos-
was asked of me and never
hat my acceptance could be
uld not have to face the way
yself. It was not uncommon for
hysically if I felt I had failed at
eone whom I thought expected

also be expressed toward other
ected such an enormous amount
room for error, I expected other
he same continual strain to achieve
and I would often become deeply
when I felt as if people were not
ulous expectations that I had set for
e and condemn others readily, and
e the appearance of grace and com-
er people at times, it was never what I
It made me angry to see others asking
hat as a weakness on the highest level,
mething I absolutely hated. I loathed
hers for help because I was afraid that
e me and condemn me for asking for

incidents such as this, gave me even more reason to feel like I had to control everything and keep my eyes wide open at all times and make myself as alert as possible in case I overlooked something that could cause destruction behind the scenes without my realizing it until it was too late.

The root of it all was a fear of overlooking things and a fear of ignorance. I could not believe that something (or someone) was all it seemed. I always felt that people and circumstances had hidden agendas that would only spring forth once I had overlooked them and judged them as being safe. I always feared that something hidden was lurking in the background, and it was just waiting for me to turn my back so that it could attack. I felt that once I had walked away from something and put it out of my mind I was vulnerable to things happening without my being aware of them and was therefore unable to stop them. As a result, my mind was constantly wired and my defenses were constantly up. I was continually alert and relaxing was nearly impossible, as I found myself unable to fully trust people or circumstances. Even feeling safe was something I struggled with, as I continually feared that I might be overlooking something that could be exploited. My relationships with others suffered greatly because of this mentality, but I felt I had no choice but to keep my guard up all the time, for whenever I tried to consciously allow myself to trust, the fear in me would simply scream louder until I obeyed what it was telling me to do.

I had no control over my own mind and over my own

thought processes, and I felt as if I lived my entire life being battered and thrown backward and forward in a sea of internal torment with no solidity or stability in sight. Every day was a challenge to get through, and often my physical health suffered due to the toll that the constant emotional stress took on my body. I began using alcohol and marijuana throughout my teenage years, as well as smoking cigarettes, more in an effort to try and release myself from the internal chaos I felt than anything else. However, marijuana did not help whatsoever and actually made things far worse.

PRIDE AND PERFECTIONISM

One of the many ways that OCD would translate itself was through a strong sense of pride. I was never one of the up front, over-the-top, and arrogant people that many would commonly associate with being prideful. The pride in my life operated through an inflated sense of responsibility and a relentless desire to do everything on my own and achieve nothing short of perfection.

Whenever anything was asked of me I always felt a powerful sense of responsibility to do more than what was asked of me. I thought that the person who had asked me was counting on me for their own sense of satisfaction and that it would come through me doing what they asked me to do absolutely perfectly. Though this was seen by many as a strong sense of workmanship and personal responsibility, in my own heart it was an entirely different matter. I was driven forward

g, upset yet feeling powerless
ent the fight was over I ran up
reds verbally for not jumping in
bout it. The reason I acted this
jected my feelings of deep-seated
tice onto her and thought in my
was somehow in control and could
g about it—but chose not to in order
r. Of course, I now realize that this
and totally unfair thing to do, as she
t as I was and didn't know what to do,
my anger and cut her out of my life as a
h we somewhat made up years later, the
as never the same. I destroyed it through
y to control my own sense of injustice and
.

ot older, my frustrations became less directed
people and more directed toward things or inan-
bjects. Looking back, I believe that I chose inani-
objects to release my rage upon, as they were not
eat to me in any way. Besides, I could justify pro-
ng my internal frustrations of crying out to cold,
artless people for justice and mercy onto inanimate
jects, as they were also heartless, seeing as they were
nanimate. I kicked holes in walls at home when I lost at
video games, smashed bits of computer equipment, and
tore items of clothing more than once.

One of the most ironic episodes happened when I
was seventeen years old and voluntarily requested an
anger management program from the school guidance

help, which was something that I felt that I deserved anyway.

The danger in this manner of thinking was the fact that the desire to succeed and achieve was never satisfied, despite what I gave them. If I had looked at these desires for what they were instead of relentlessly trying to fulfill them I would have realized that even if I had gained the entire world, I would still not have been satisfied. The only difference now was that seeing as I had achieved everything, I had nothing left to medicate that desire with, so now I was stuck with all the achievements in the world and a heart filled with nothing but dissatisfaction. Of course, I could not see this at the time, and so I set about doing everything I could to try and fulfill what I felt was expected of me anyway.

This mind-set was hard to define, as it was also very subtle. It would translate through people asking me to do things that needed to be done, or that were genuinely expected of me by others, such as within the workplace. My natural state of mind would be to rush to do what was asked of me, as it was something that was expected of me anyway. I could then justify my driven mentality because what was being asked of me was something I was being asked to do in my job. Though what was being asked of me was not wrong, the driven mentality in my life that I acted on to achieve it was wrong. I needed to do what was asked of me at work, but my heart was out of balance. If I was confronted about my inability to do something at work that was asked of me, it was very easy for me to collapse into a pit of depression. Being confronted for failing to achieve at work was not wrong by any means, but beating myself up mentally for feeling as if I had failed everyone and myself for being unable to fulfill my own over-inflated expectations was very wrong indeed.

I felt as if I was completely alone, without anyone who cared about me or was standing beside me, prepared to catch me if I fell. Although this was not the case in reality, I could not see past this belief in my own mind. Some people need to hit rock bottom before they can truly change for the better, as they need to explore the depths of the darkest parts of themselves before they can ever really appreciate the easier times in life. I was (and to some degree, still am) one of those people. The problem for me is that I believed so strongly I had to be self-sufficient that I simply could not allow myself to hit any kind of bottom. I was terrified of what was there and also terrified that I would be thrown out and rejected for no longer being the super strong person able to cope with anything. I feared I would be shown up as weak and inferior and that I would be vulnerable to the mercy and judgment of others, which was something I feared so much I would do anything to avoid it.

This inflated self-expectation and pride resulted in a lonely and miserable way of life for me. I often found myself physically exhausted due to the huge amount I demanded of myself, and of course my physical exhaustion would lead to health problems, which would then bring forth strong feelings of condemnation on my part for being sick and unable to perform. What I feared was counselor. She gave me a cassette tape to listen to on the subject, so I took it home and put it in my Walkman with the idea of listening to it lying on my bed. For whatever reason the tape jammed and broke the Walkman. Seconds later the Walkman, with the jammed tape still in it, went flying across the room and was smashed to smithereens against the wall, leaving me worse off than I was originally.

I tried to hide this behavior as I got older and I began to realize just how destructive it was and how easily I could destroy friendships and relationships due to this problem I could not solve. I struggled to engage in healthy confrontation with other people—even when I needed to—because I felt that I could not express my views in a confrontational and potentially hostile environment without these enormous frustrations surfacing and taking over my behavior, as they so often did during my childhood. If I felt as if I needed something from the person I was confronting, such as an employer, I would do everything I could to bury this behavior so that it could not come out and potentially destroy something that I could not get by without, like my pay check.

If I allowed this sense of frustration and rage against injustice to infiltrate my responses when engaged in a confrontational situation, they would quickly take over, and I would lose the ability to control the anger. I would just keep heaping on more and more of it until the other person or party backed down. What really frightened me about this was the absolute lack of limit to the anger. It was almost like falling into a black hole that would take me straight down to hell itself. I knew that if I threatened to subdue someone with violence the threats were not empty and that I was more than willing and capable of fulfilling them. I always knew that when I got into that headspace I could have seriously injured someone in a fight—or worse. I was never a bulky person physically, but as they say it's the size of the fight in the dog, not the dog in the fight.

Big portions of my life were spent trying very hard to cover up this behavior and pretend it wasn't there—even going so far as to block it out and live completely in denial of its existence. Confrontational and hostile situations were to be avoided at all costs, as I did not want to have to face the fact that my frustration and anger would consume me completely and could land me in a lot of trouble very easily. Living in denial did not solve the problem, of course. However, it was the only way I felt I could live with this beast I carried within me.

Dissatisfaction and the Need to Run

The issues in my life would translate very strongly for me in the way of constant dissatisfaction with my environment and surroundings. Nothing was ever good enough for me, and I was always looking for the next thing: the next thrill, the next relationship, the next distraction. Although this seemed like a perfectly understandable way to live at the time, it really wasn't living at all, as I was not really enjoying anything and continually dissatisfied with everything I had. Every time I got something

I wanted, I would find a way to be dissatisfied with that too and move on to the next desire. I was not aware that the actual answer I was looking for was not external but within myself, and instead of trying to satisfy the emotional pressure with more "things," which I thought would fulfill it, I needed to take a look at the root of the problem. However, the root of the problem was too painful to face, so it was easier to just try and cover it up.

One example of this was the way that I handled my money. Spending money almost became addictive, as there was constantly a new rush that came from buying something new. It represented a change of sorts from the normal way of things and gave me something to take my mind off my own personal issues. Once the thrill of one new purchase wore off the simple answer was to go out and look for something else to buy. Thanks to my own reckless spending I managed to get myself into some financial trouble. At one point I was paying off a loan of $5,000, plus a student loan of $7,000, with a maxed out credit card with a $2,000 limit and $1,000 of overdraft.

Although initially I was able to cover everything up and keep everything within me subdued and controlled through the possession or relationship, as time went on they began to lose their ability to distract me from myself, and I would begin to lose interest and need something else. This was incredibly dangerous—both for myself and others, as relationships were often built on how I could distract myself from my own feelings instead of any kind of genuine love and appreciation for the other person or honest appraisal of a current circumstance.

Once they were unable to bring me the happiness that I craved, I would very often throw both people and otherwise good circumstances out of my life and blame them for pushing me away, when in fact it was my own feelings and refusal to acknowledge them that actually destroyed everything.

This boredom that would set in would constantly bring about an attitude of complaining and unhappiness. I could be in the best possible position—for example, working in a great job, living in a nice house, and being surrounded by good friends—yet I would still find every reason under the sun to complain and would project my internal misery and dissatisfaction onto my environment and others around me. I would often find fault with other people and judge them harshly out of my own dissatisfaction with life, and I would often end up ruining good situations due to the darkness I carried within myself.

I had a vision once of a man who was sitting in a chair with his arms and legs shackled to the chair, with an empty chair next to him. The man constantly complained about the fact that he was stuck to this chair and that he hated it, that he was desperately unhappy, and that he needed to be in the other chair. He complained and complained and never gave anyone a moment's peace about it, until finally the shackles opened up and the man was able to walk free of the chair that he was in. However, the parts of the shackles that were holding his arms did not open; the only shackles that opened were the ones that were holding on to the chair. He got up and moved, but he took his shackles with him. Once he sat down the shackles he carried with him simply clamped down shut onto the chair that he had moved to—and the whole process started all over again.

The man I saw in the chair was me, and the chairs represented different circumstances in my life that I was continually jumping to and from in order to try and satisfy my emotional needs. This was a very cowardly way of life, as it constantly revolved around shirking blame and responsibilities and trying to take the easy way out. When the going got tough, I would get going—out of there as fast as I could, without realizing that I was taking the problem with me wherever I went. It would then just be a matter of time until the same problems began to surface—albeit with a different face. Then the whole process would start all over again, and I would be left craving a plateau of "happiness" that never seemed to come.

THE VICTIM MENTALITY

I suffered from a so-called victim mentality throughout my entire life, which was reinforced by some experiences of over-discipline in my childhood years. Some people seemed to be able to sense that there was something about me that allowed them to mistreat me as much as they wanted in the knowledge that they could get away with this injustice. It was almost as if I gave off subconscious messages to those around me, which were saying to others, "Go on, abuse me, slap me around, mistreat me. It doesn't matter how much you hurt me or upset me, I will never show it, and I will never fight back. I deserve this. You can do whatever you like to me, and I promise not to fight back. You are completely free of any kind of consequence if you attack me, and you can show the darkest and ugliest side of yourself toward me that you like. I promise I will not fight you or try and stand up to you if you do this to me."

I remember when I was only about five years old I was walking through a shopping mall one day. A child about my own age came toward me in the other direction, and for no reason at all he hit me as I walked past him. I didn't engage him in any way, yet he struck me. The anger exploded through my being toward the boy; however, I did nothing except bottle it up and repress it. This created a furious anger toward myself for allowing such an injustice to happen and for allowing others to treat me as if I was so insignificant and not worth anything. However, I would just bottle that anger up as well.

This was to be a reoccurring theme in my life. It didn't matter where I went or how I tried to act, people seemed to know that they could abuse me both physically and verbally without any fear of consequences. I hated these people with a powerful hatred for doing this and ignoring the conscience of their own hearts, but more than anything I hated myself for not being able to fight back, and I hated the bonds that kept me tied down into this victim-orientated state of mind. I felt confused, angry, and frustrated, as it seemed to me that no matter what I did, nothing seemed to change this. Whenever anyone spoke toward me in an overpowering manner, it was almost like there was something whispering in my ear telling me that I deserved what they were doing to me and that I should let them get away with what they were doing, as it was the right thing to do and that trying to stand up to them would be wrong.

I felt powerless to do anything, for I felt that the moment I tried to engage in something, someone or something would come along and try to take control of me and what I was doing. I felt as if I had no free will and could only ever live a life where my every action was controlled and forced to fit into the will of others. It got to the point where I was afraid to try and attempt to do things—especially when it came to situations where I needed to stand up for myself—because I feared that I would be "put back in my place." For me the message was, "You can't do that. You aren't allowed to act that way. You don't have any clout or any authority. There's no reason why anyone should listen to you!" These internal forces were so powerful I felt that I had to obey them at all costs, so I went out of my way to stop myself from getting into situations where I could potentially be controlled by other people, just to avoid having to face this issue.

The hold this had on my life was huge. Situations where I was experiencing bullying of any kind—usually at school—felt like they were beyond hopeless, as I simply could not get out. The more I tried to find it within myself to fight back, the more these powerful internal forces rallied up against me, so I ended up just bowing down to the abuse and letting it happen. Of course, the more I let it happen, the more anger I developed toward myself and the internal chains that held me prisoner. I felt very strongly that there was no way out for me. I felt that my whole life was completely at the mercy of those who did not care about me, and whether or not I suffered throughout the day was up to another person. The only thing I could hope for was that perhaps someday I could find a situation where bullying and hostile behavior were not present so I could therefore be safe. However, this proved to be impossible, as everywhere I went throughout my life, different situations would trigger these issues in my life.

I felt as if I could do nothing except run away from these issues, so I retreated further and further into myself as time went on, filling my mind with distractions to take my thoughts away from the reality that was destroying my life. This mentality would cause me to continually want to move around in the hope of finding somewhere that I considered "safe." In fact, all the while I was simply taking the issue with me wherever I went. Situations that I once considered happy and enjoyable became miserable the moment that these issues were triggered, and it caused me to throw away some good situations in my life simply because they had shown me up for what I really was. However, I didn't know what else I could do—except run.

THE NEED TO CONTROL THINGS THROUGH PASSIVE BEHAVIOR

A huge contributor to my victim mentality was the fear of the unknown. I was terrified of what I did not know and could not predict, and I never learned how to handle this adequately. Whenever I found myself facing a situation that I did not know or understand completely, I would tend to react out of fear, and more often than not the fear I acted out of drove me to act in a highly passive manner to try to prevent the bad things from happening to me that I did not feel that I could handle.

The outworking of fear in my life was very complicated and resulted in highly unpredictable behavior. Early on I began to fear authority and people with any kind of power over me, whether it was physical, through social standings, or otherwise. I felt that the way to keep myself safe when faced with this kind of fear was to bow down and let others walk all over me. I found it immensely difficult to stand up to them, as everything inside me kept telling me that I would be safe and would keep the peace if I just obeyed and just let them push me around. I therefore became the stereotypical victim for bullies, especially throughout my time at school.

My honest belief with this mentality was that by being super nice, willing to bend over backward for absolutely everyone, and sacrificing my own needs and rights for the sake of others I would appeal to the good side of the people in the situation that I was facing. I could therefore control the outcome of it to make it into a safe environment for myself. I dove headfirst into this mentality and began using it in all aspects of my life and did absolutely everything I could to avoid any kind of confrontation. The fear that contributed to this was the feeling of not being able to trust others and what might happen to me if I were to incite their anger through my actions. I literally did not know or trust what others were capable of.

Looking back I also now believe that I was aware of the depth of the rage and desire for revenge within myself, and I was afraid that others may have those same things in their lives to the same extent that I did, only without the fear that kept it bound up. My honest belief of others was that they would do anything to win an argument or fight, no matter what. I felt that they would do anything they possibly could to defeat me in an argument or fight and that I just had no chance of winning.

I also did not trust myself in these situations. I did not feel like a strong person, nor did I feel that I could handle what was thrown at me if someone came at me with anger. I felt like I could not control my own emotions and that if I were to use my own anger in a conflict with others, the situation would quickly snowball. My need to control the situation and be able to handle it would get to a point that I simply could not contain it, and I was afraid I would quite literally snap and go insane—lost without hope within my own mind. I did not feel that others would listen to me and that I would receive respect for standing up for myself. I felt that others saw me as I saw myself, weak and not worthy of respect or acknowledgment. So I gave up the battle before even engaging in it because I knew that I had already lost. The only way I felt that I could win any sort of argument in my life was to sacrifice everything to appease the good side of the forces that stood against me so that they would do what I wanted without abusing me.

This passive, fear-based mentality was all built on lies and the outworking of this nearly destroyed me. I became filled with rage and hatred toward those who confronted me and took advantage of what I held within myself, yet when the opportunity came to confront them I would simply retreat back into my shell, because trying to confront and fight them was terrifying. The fear got worse the more I tried to push myself into confrontation, so I ended up with tremendous internal rage and frustration. This was aimed at the people who took advantage of my fear-based prison, but also a lot was toward myself and my prison of fear that kept me bound. My rage had no outlet, so it just sat there and festered.

THE NEED TO CONTROL THINGS THROUGH AGGRESSION AND INTIMIDATION

However, there was another side to these fears. Sometimes I felt I could bully another person. This was because I sensed that their weakness and fear was greater than my own. Then the passive behavior would all of a sudden flick into reverse, and I would become the complete opposite—aggressive, cruel, cold, and relentless. I was finally getting some sort of an outlet that I believed to be non-threatening for the pain I had within myself, and I no longer needed to be passive. I had power, so I could be as aggressive, condescending, and belittling as I liked. The difference in this instance was that when I was the one being bullied, the suffering that was caused was right in my face, as I was the one who was experiencing it, and I could not run and hide from it. However, when I was doing the bullying I was free to completely ignore the pain I was causing others and didn't have to face up to it, simply because I was not the one being victimized. And as the other person was too weak to fight me, I wasn't going to have to face it. When I was the victim I felt as if I had no choice in the matter except to suffer. However, when I was the bully—whether or not another person suffered was my choice, and I liked that feeling of power and control.

Because I was so focused on my own feelings of victimization from previous experiences, when I was presented with a position of power over another person I would abuse that power through disrespect and selfishness. It wasn't even that I deliberately wanted to cause them suffering; it was just that it was irrelevant because there was no chance that they would ever confront me and throw it back into my face. Therefore, through my own self-pity, ignorance, and selfishness, I became one of the people that I despised so much, and I caused others to suffer in the same way that I had suffered. I felt that my own life had been wrecked through the carelessness and ignorance of others, and my anger at this caused me to hurt other people out of my carelessness and ignorance. I did not think of how I might be hurting other people and put myself first in everything. My anger at the pain I felt through the ignorance of others caused me to be ignorant of people around me and to cause them the same pain.

This was how I learned about how bullies and their victims function, through being on both sides of the situation. Bullies are completely unconcerned about the plight of their victims and do not give the suffering they deliberately cause a second thought. Often, this is due to them being bullied themselves, and the neglect and abuse that they experienced now translates into the neglect and abuse they give to other people. When I was bullying others, I still felt like a victim myself; it was the rage of the victim mentality within me that drove me to bullying others, as I saw it as an emotional release. Of course it did not help. Bullying others was never going to heal the pain I felt within myself. I felt a powerful sense of self-loathing, as I knew that I was embracing the same cowardly behavior as those who had bullied me. However, seeing as I was able to identify the target as being weaker than myself, they became my outlet for my self-hatred as well, which of course made the anger I felt toward myself worse, and the spiral would continue.

My actions had consequences—both for myself and others. Through only focusing on the wrong that was done to me and completely ignoring the fear that caused me to let people treat me so disrespectfully to begin with,

I became very self-righteous. Friendships were often strained due to my behavior, and relationships, especially with girls, failed regularly. I became very angry whenever relationships failed and would inevitably blame the person on the other end of the relationship, and I would justify this blame by finding things they had done wrong, while completely ignoring what part of me had caused this to happen as well. The deep-seated knot of anger and confusion, coming from a fear-based existence, was seeping its way through into other areas of my life, and the depth of what I held within my own heart was revealing itself through my circumstances.

Though in a way I was justified at being angry at others for abusing and bullying me since what they did was undoubtedly wrong, only focusing on that anger and ignoring the other areas of my life and my own personal responsibilities was not helping anyone at all, least of all me. My subconscious belief was, "I shouldn't have to look at the other side of the story. I shouldn't have to look in the mirror and see if any part of this was actually my doing. What they did was wrong. End of story." Though this was very often true, it was only ever part of the story. However, this is the only part I would choose to focus on, and because there was only a realization of part of the truth—and not the whole picture—I would find no peace with this way of thinking. The internal conflict of the deep-seated knowledge that I had also done wrong but would not admit it to anyone caused a powerful frustration in my life that affected nearly everything I did.

REJECTION

For as long as I can remember I struggled with powerful feelings of rejection. I always felt that I did not fit in with other people and that I was somehow different from them. I felt as if I was deliberately excluded from social circles and that my presence was not welcome among my peers. These feelings would come through in my attitudes toward others. As a child, friendships meant very little to me, and the moment that somebody did something wrong in my eyes, I would throw them out of my life without so much as a second thought. I would not give them a chance to explain themselves, and I never had any interest in trying to restore the relationship. Once I said it was over, it was over forever and nothing would change that.

I was often perceived as having a hostile and uncaring attitude toward those around me due to the rejection I carried within my own heart. My subconscious belief was that the world had turned against me and was trying its best to throw me out and get rid of me, so I decided in my disgust to turn against the world. People found me to be unapproachable, over-emotional, and volatile. The older I got, the more I learned to repress these feelings. I did everything in my power to put myself in circumstances where these feelings could not be triggered. However, the unresolved rejection was like a crushing black weight on my soul from which I could find no lasting release.

These unresolved feelings had a profound effect on my

personal relationships with those whom I was close to such as family members. I did not believe it when other people told me that they cared about me. I felt as if they were lying and that they were trying to manipulate me into a place of vulnerability so that they could exploit it and attack me once my defenses had been lowered. I continually second-guessed people and viewed them suspiciously. The moment they did something that reinforced what I already believed about them (e.g., they lost their temper), I would say to myself, "Ha! I knew it! They aren't a good person at all. They're just a monster in disguise, same as me. I've found out just how fake they are. My suspicions were justified. I'm so glad I learned this now!" I enjoyed my rebellion, and I found reason to be disappointed in nearly every person I was ever in any sort of relationship with throughout my life.

The older I became the more I realized that childish power trips and outbursts of emotion were not well looked upon. However, I did not deal with my behavior; instead, I sought to repress it within myself and try to distance myself from what I really was. Of course, nothing had really changed. I was still the disconnected, cold, and violent individual I had always been. However, I was now doing the best I could to ignore the truth about myself and pack it down so tightly that no one would ever know about it. That way, I figured, perhaps I could somehow stumble my way through life.

I would often find myself in relationships with people that I was forced to be dependent on to some degree, for example, coworkers, flat mates, or neighbors. I knew subconsciously that if the monster of rejection within me was triggered, it would definitely send the relationship spiraling out of control into irreparable destruction. I thought that the moment I showed who I really was people would throw me out instantly, just as I had done to so many other people over the years. I could not allow this to happen, as I knew that I needed the relationship in some regard, so I would retreat into a fearful mentality that enabled others to treat me as badly as they liked. I would let them do it, as I felt so strongly that if I tried to fight back they would just throw me out without question, and I would be left without something that I needed, with no one to blame for losing it but myself. I controlled people, circumstances, and situations as much as I could to prevent any of this from happening to me.

I became a fake person. People saw me as a kind and gentle person, but it was really nothing but a cover-up for my true self that I had created out of fear. I put on this mask so as to never give others a chance to see who I really was and therefore reject me. I hated who I really was at heart. I knew that others would too, as I had no comprehension at the time of grace and compassion for others, even when it was offered to me. So much energy went into trying to contain this issue I carried within me, and it left me with little hope for the future, as I could see nothing good through the black cloud that hung over me and clouded my vision.

OPPRESSION

For as long as I can remember I struggled with a powerful sense of oppression. I always felt as if there were two people inside me at any one time. One of them was me, and the other one was almost like a monster that towered over me and was continually looking me right in the eyes with a sense of hostility and violence. When I tried to say something, this other person would disagree immediately, simply so that it could stand against me. Anything that I tried to do, it continually put pressure on me and told me that what I was doing was wrong. There was no escape from this hostile opposition, and I felt as if I could never rest, as if I ever let go and just let myself fully relax, I would give this monster the power to destroy me and everything around me.

This oppression would oppose me in anything and everything it got the chance to use against me. For example, if someone was to mistreat me, it would come up with every possible reason that it could to justify what that person had done to me and make it sound believable. I would be continually bombarded with this from within, and the more I tried to ignore and overlook it, the stronger the bombardment became until I felt as if I had no choice but to give in to it. This was a big reason why I found it very hard to stand up for myself. The moment I tried to fight back against someone or something, the oppression would rise up against me and beat me down until I had no choice but to quit.

Other people's arguments against me would be

reinforced by the oppression that came from within, even if their arguments were not based in fact and I was actually in the right. If I ever tried to speak out against anything that I felt was wrong, the oppression would immediately rise up against me and do the best it could to choke my voice in my throat to the point where I couldn't get the words out. This would manifest physically for me. I sometimes struggled very much to get the words out when I was talking, especially in a situation that involved any sort of confrontation.

This oppression would translate into a furious hatred for anyone whom I felt was trying to oppress me or stand against me in any way. Someone might be disagreeing with me in an argument or standing against me for behaving in a way that was out of line. Their actions (even though they may have been completely justified) would trigger the oppression that I carried within myself, which would tell me that they just wanted to keep me down and keep me under their thumb where I belonged so that they could have the satisfaction of controlling and bullying someone else. It would tell me that the person standing against me was completely evil through and through and that the only way out was to destroy them with violence and aggression. None of this was true, of course, as there was no way I could tell what was really happening in the heart of another person, but the depth and subtlety of this voice made it very difficult to ignore. However, I could not express the rage, as the second I felt it, the oppression would kick in again and tell me that there was no way I could overcome the person that I was facing. The rage had nowhere left to go but within, where it would slowly start to destroy me from the inside.

Due to the influence of this continual internal oppression and opposition, I felt as if I had no voice in life and that I could not change anything. I felt as if no one listened to me and that I was not respected or cared about. I felt unimportant and continually stifled. It felt as if I was thrashing about in a padded room, trying to take charge of something, trying to change something, but the more I thrashed the stronger the oppression seemed to stand against me, preventing me from doing anything. Due to its refusal to back down, I eventually felt as if I had no choice but to submit to defeat, even though I was not happy about it at all. A huge issue of rage, despair, and frustration was growing inside me through the oppression that ruled my life. The more it squashed me from within, the deeper and more powerful the frustration became.

Most of my daily behavior came out of an effort to keep this issue restrained within me by doing my best to control circumstances and interpersonal relationships, mainly through using timid and passive behavior. The moment that I ever did something that I perceived could make me vulnerable in any way I went into a state of perpetual anxiety and fear. It felt almost as if I was scared that the oppression I felt from within was going to strike me down simply for doing something without its authorization. I felt as if I could do nothing outside of the strict boundaries it had set for me and that my every move revolved around trying to please this internal monster so that it would not abuse me. The important thing to note here was that there was never really any sort of treatment that I received from others throughout my life that caused me to feel like this. This was something that had a hold on me for as long as I can remember, and I cannot think of any particular situation that could have caused it to begin.

This monster of oppression strongly affected my work and my interpersonal relationships. I found it incredibly difficult to trust people and enjoy any sort of situation I found myself in. I was not respected at my places of employment due to the vibes I gave off, and when I was pushed hard enough it would translate through aggression and abuse toward people around me. It would only become a matter of time before I destroyed every situation I was in due to the depth of the evil that was within my own heart, which caused me to want to move on to new things in the hope that things would improve. Of course, simply changing circumstances would never solve the root of the problem and would simply add to the hopeless cycle of dissatisfaction and unhappiness I continually found myself in.

DEPRESSION

These powerful emotional issues in my life translated into a very deep depression. I spent most of my days feeling as if I were walking around carrying a ton of bricks inside my soul, without any real idea as to how I would handle whatever I would have to face throughout the day. I was diagnosed with clinical depression in my early twenties and was advised to begin taking antidepressant medication. However, although that took the edge off the way I was feeling it was not really a solution for me, only a mask to help cover up and manage the true problems I was experiencing.

I would wake up in the mornings and immediately feel overwhelmed by an onslaught of heavy emotions. I was aware to some extent of the depth of what was happening within me and the issues that gave rise to the depression, but that awareness was only on a subconscious level. I would just overlook the pain in my conscious mind, which would make the depression worse, as I knew deep down that I was not facing the facts that I needed to face about my life.

Depression affected nearly every aspect of my life. Most of my time and energy was spent trying to minimize the effects of depression. I mainly tried to do this through trying to control the actions of others and my circumstances in order to stop anything from happening to me that could have sent me spiraling downhill into an emotional black hole.

It also affected the way that I was perceived by other people. I remember watching a video that had been filmed of my Cub Scout brigade when I was very young. While watching the video, I noticed a child in the corner by himself with a very downcast expression on his face. He appeared to be miserable and not enjoying himself at all. I wondered who this child was. It took me a few moments to realize that it was me.

One of the ways depression would translate in my life was toward those I felt that I could overpower and control, such as children (as I became older) or people I felt were scared of me in some regard. I would often treat these people with a cold, borderline hostile attitude and a sense of indignation. It was like I felt that I didn't have to pretend anymore, so I simply sat and let everything hang out in the open in a place where I did not have to make excuses for it, and in doing this I would project my misery onto others. I have heard the quote before about certain people who could be "an angel in public and a demon in private." I fitted this category perfectly, as I would completely switch my behavior when I felt that I was able to do so.

When it came to people I felt I could control and overpower, it was almost like I was having a conversation with myself in my subconscious mind between my conscience and the depression that plagued my life. These two sides seemed to be continually at war within my heart and emotions. Due to my own refusal to look inward I ignored the raging battles within in the hope that they would go away, which only ever made things worse. The conversation usually followed this thought pattern:

> *Conscience:* "You are not treating this person as they deserve. You are acting toward them the

same way that you hate other people acting toward you."

Depression: "I don't care. They are weaker than me and cannot fight back. They can't make me face this, so there is no reason why I shouldn't treat them badly out of my own negativity. No one can stop me."

Conscience: "Well, I don't approve. This isn't the right thing to do. You know this."

Depression: "I don't care if you don't approve. I'm not in the business of thinking about other people and their needs. All I ever need to think about is mine. So I'm going to ignore you."

Conscience: "If you choose to ignore me, you will have no peace in your life. Nothing will make you feel better. You will not get any peace or satisfaction out of anything. Everything will only make you feel worse—even the things that you love. I'm not going to back down on this."

Depression: "I don't care. I'm still going to ignore you and get away with it circumstantially and find a way to justify my behavior."

This would usually be followed up with me trying to do something to medicate the depression. It was usually something that I enjoyed that would help me take my mind off things such as video games or alcohol. Of course, nothing ever really solved the problem, and the depression only continued to get worse. The worse the depression got, the less I enjoyed my distractions. The less I enjoyed my distractions, the more I became embittered and angry with life and everything in it, as I felt that everything was letting me down.

A New Sense of Hope: the Journey Begins

Living in this manner was simply not sustainable. I struggled to sleep most nights, and I would spend my days living in fear and dread. I held no hope for my future and would often wonder if my next day on Earth was going to be my last. There was nothing to look forward to in life and nothing to ever be able to truly enjoy and appreciate. Though I had gone to church on and off throughout the years, I had never really got much out of it.

One day, after a particularly bad relationship break up, I decided to go along to church with my mother. I did something I had not done in a long time: I walked to the front of the church and admitted that I could not carry the heavy burdens of the life I had been living any longer and that I needed help. The usher was very kind and compassionate and prayed for me. He then told me that God had a plan for my life and that He was going to use me to touch the lives of others. That was the first time I ever felt that my life had meaning. I knew at that point, in an instant, that my life's mission from there on in was to follow God, as He would have the answers for me.

I immediately found a new lease on life and a deep-seated sense of excitement and joy. Committing myself to God completely changed my attitude. However, it was not going to be the ride that I was expecting. On the one hand, my spirit had been made whole through the blood of Christ and therefore restored to life. On the other hand, my soul was still crammed full of the pain and darkness that had come from years of emotional and spiritual self-neglect, as well as substance use and deeply rooted unresolved issues. Though the joy at finding this new lease on life was apparent, the darkness in my soul was always lurking just under the surface.

I had a vision of the spiritual journey that was ahead of me. I saw myself standing at the foot of a cliff. There was an amazing view from the top of this cliff. I could see beautiful scenery all around, including an amazing sunset. Far off in the distance I saw a high peak, about the same height as the one that I was currently standing on. That peak, I sensed, had a view far more amazing than the one that I was standing on. I knew in the deepest core of my heart that the peak I could see up ahead was where I wanted to be, and most importantly, where God wanted to take me.

The cliff I was on had a very steep drop, and I could see the bottom far, far below me. The bottom of the cliff was shrouded in deep darkness, though I could scarcely make out objects in the darkness that looked like boulders and walls. This darkness stretched on for miles, and there were these objects shrouded in the darkness as far along as I could see. The darkness only stopped once it got to the bottom of the other peak that I could see far off in the distance.

The peak I was standing on was symbolic for the place I found myself in right after I rededicated my life to Christ—joy and happiness at having rededicated my life to the One who created me. The steep drop symbolized how quickly my mood would fall once I truly grasped what was ahead of me, and the darkened valley full of boulders and walls was the spiritual wilderness I was going to have to walk through in order to face my problems head on and deal with them rather than trying to avoid them, as I had done for so long. It was not going to be easy, and the time spent in the darkened valley was not going to be short, as it was designed to clear the darkness out of the deepest areas of my soul. This would take time, endurance, and patience.

My mind at the time refused to accept that I would have to face this, as I expected that God would go along with how I had journeyed through life up until this point and that God would help me to keep on running. I expected that God would just put a bridge over that dark valley so that I would be spared the pain of having to walk through it.

I had my entire life planned out to the letter, and I expected God to help me to fulfill what I thought was best for me. I wanted God to be my servant along my journey and do what I wanted Him to do with me. Little did I know God was not in the business of being put into anybody's pockets—least of all mine.

Part Two

LEARNING TO HEAL

RELEASE THROUGH HONESTY

ISHONESTY HAD CHARACTERIZED my entire emotional and spiritual life up till this point. I was never straight up with people, would always take the easy way out, and would lie and manipulate my way out of pretty much everything so that I could continue to run. I was about to receive a real wake-up call from God that if I was going to be one of His children, then I needed to stop this fiasco of living a life with a thousand different masks and would have to start learning to get honest and real. Although I did not realize it at the time, it was a wake-up call that I desperately needed.

My prayer life as a new Christian started off being one saying that everything was fine and I was so happy about everything, while I was completely ignoring the depth of what was going on within me. However, inside, I was deeply unhappy with my life, as I was not enjoying the university course I was studying, and I was not enjoying the part-time job I was doing. My attitude began to disintegrate further over time as the pressure didn't let off like I was expecting it to, and I did not know what to do with how I was feeling at the time. This heaviness began to manifest itself in my outward behavior, and I began to develop a very poor attitude at my workplace.

One day I was abused by a customer, who took offense to my attitude. This affected me very deeply, as it dredged up a lot within me I had never really faced before, and I didn't know how to handle it. In the past I would just bottle my emotions up and run to the next distraction; however, God would not let this happen, and this event just would not leave my mind. I was aware of a huge heaviness within me, which had been triggered by this situation.

Throughout all this I maintained a fake prayer life with God, telling Him that everything was fine and that I was happy. Surprisingly enough, my prayer life was not effective, and if I were honest, I didn't even really believe what I was telling God anyway. I thought that this was what God wanted to hear, as I thought that God expected me to be good, so I tried to be as good as possible. It didn't help. Due to the constant internal pressure I began to feel more and more burdened until I began to learn to truly unload my burdens at the feet of God.

One night when the situation at work was still fresh in my mind, I was writing something in a notebook and all of a sudden all the bile and anger and fury started exploding out of me onto the page. It felt good, as the pressure was finally being released, so I continued to let it out—except this time it was based in prayer. However, it was not the same as before. My prayers were now honest and were detailing exactly what I was truly going through. And they were ugly, vile, and spiteful prayers, as they were loaded with the emotions I had been suppressing for so long. However, I did not feel guilty or condemned by God as I expected to. I felt better through doing it, as I had begun my journey of honest prayer and began to develop an honest relationship with God.

This was something that was really new to me. I thought God only wanted to hear shallow, happy prayers. However, I have learned that God appreciates it far more when we are honest with Him, regardless of what it is about. And that honesty is not always pretty. I found myself literally screaming and yelling at God at times in prayer just trying to describe what was happening within me. Those prayers were ugly. But, more importantly, they were honest. Praying them began to lift a heavy burden off my shoulders.

This was only the beginning of this journey, and with hindsight I am glad this situation occurred, as it pushed me into learning about a healthy prayer life. I felt God continually leading me to talk with Him honestly about what was happening to me. I embraced this thoroughly, because it began to bring me relief. Since God had come into my life, old feelings and the powerful emotional strongholds from my past were beginning to surface, as God wanted to change me from within. Some days were consumed with these powerful, negative emotions, but as they did I began to find solace in dumping them all on God's shoulders.

God wants His people to be happy and joyful; however, that needs to come out of a changed heart. Hearts change through honesty, not fakeness, and for me learning to be honest involved learning about discernment.

RELEASE THROUGH DISCERNMENT

I remember one particular day when the seismic change in my thinking began to take place and I began to develop a true awareness of what was happening within me. I was living at home with my parents and working full-time in a supermarket, and though I enjoyed the job my time was approaching to leave, as I had made the decision to attend Bible college. I was excited about the prospect of change and looking forward to moving away from home for the first time.

During one particular week I began to notice a change in my sleeping patterns. I found it harder to get to sleep than usual. To paint a metaphorical picture of what was beginning to happen to me, it was almost as if there was a light switched on inside my brain that was just too bright, and I could not turn it off so that I could sleep. It wasn't a peaceful light—more like trying to sleep in a room with the lights blazing at full blast. And the lights could not be shut off, as they were designed to deprive someone of sleep.

Usually when things like this happened in the past

they would gradually pass in the course of a few days, and I would begin to start sleeping normally again. However, this time it was not the case. Over the next two nights I progressively slept less and less, and by the time the third night came around I was awake for nearly the entire night, apart from about two hours when I finally managed to get a bit of restless sleep. I was totally exhausted.

I had been told that quoting Scripture was a good way to bring about change for the better in a person's life, so throughout that third night I began to quote the verse over and over again, like, God "grants sleep to those he loves" (Ps. 127:2). However, it had no effect, and that feeling of a bright light switched on inside me that wouldn't shut off continued to keep me awake. I tried everything I could think of to get to sleep. I tried sleeping pills, alcohol, listening to gentle music in the background, taking covers off, putting more covers on—and still sleep did not come. I went to work after sleeping two hours completely exhausted before I even began my day of work. My parents told me that I should sleep really heavily the following night; however, I knew that something was wrong, and unless something changed I had no idea when I would be able to sleep next.

As the day went by I began to think and pray and ask God what was happening. As I did this I began to think about this horrible bright light within me. The more I thought about it, the more I became aware of it and the worse I felt. But I felt the Spirit of God leading me to think about it, almost as if He were saying, *"This is where you will find your answer.*" I began to try to discern and put into words exactly what I was feeling. Suddenly the words came to me: "*slavery, captivity, bondage, control.*" I rebuked these four words in the name of Jesus Christ, and it was like that horrible, tormenting light that kept me awake against my will went out. I came home that night and slept heavily.

I soon realized that something deeply embedded within my heart had been having a huge effect on my outward circumstances and that once my heart changed, my outward circumstances changed also. I realized at this point that if I were truly to find peace I would need to learn to journey through what I was feeling and get to know what was happening within me rather than trying to run away from it, as I had always done previously. God had allowed this to surface in my life to teach me a valuable lesson. In His eyes, three practically sleepless nights were insignificant compared to the value of the lesson He was teaching me through this circumstance. It would serve me for years to come.

LEARNING ABOUT SPIRITUAL TIES FROM GENERATIONAL LINES

As I learned about discernment I began to develop more of an awareness of the spiritual realm. There was a lot more at work in my life behind the scenes than I realized, and through trying to control everything externally and take my mind off them all I was doing was giving the true sources to my struggles room to grow and fester.

One such example that I learned about came from an experience I had a few years back. As I began to move into my teenage years, I realized that one of the main things expected of teenage males was to obtain their driver's license. Most of my peers did this easily; however, it was never something I was good at. I struggled very much to learn to drive, and even once I had the basics and was able to drive on the road I was not confident while driving. I did not enjoy being behind the wheel at all. I barely passed my restricted driver's license, and when I eventually went for my full driver's license I failed the test. People told me it was just a confidence thing and that it would pass with time and practice, but I just never seemed to get any better at it. This was an enormous cause of frustration in my life, as I wanted my own independence, and I was tired of having to rely on other people and public transport to get myself around. Yet, I just felt like I couldn't get a vehicle or my driver's license, and I didn't know why.

I started a new job in a new city, and I was able to take my pushbike from where I was living at the time to my place of work; however, my current living situation was not ideal, and my flat mates were very keen to move. This really jammed me in between a rock and a hard place. There were very few places available nearby my work that I could walk or ride my pushbike to, so I would have to look at finding other ways. But I still felt so restricted internally that I was unable to get a vehicle.

I knew this would have to change at some point, as I could not continue to rely on public transport and other people forever; yet, I could not see how it was going to happen.

Out of frustration I wrote about my struggles regarding this to my mother, who is very insightful and has had a lot of experience with prayer. She set some time aside and prayed for me in this matter. Later on she told me that she felt God had shown her that I had inherited a fear of driving and a fear of motor vehicle accidents, which had come down spiritually through other people in my family. At first I thought this was very strange that I could have this fear, as I had never had an accident in my life and had never seen one. There was no justifiable reasoning for this fear to exist in my heart, yet it gripped me very powerfully regardless of my previous experiences.

Shortly afterward the strangest thing happened for me. I felt very strongly that I should get a motorcycle, and about a month or so later I purchased my first motorcycle and set about learning to ride it. I thoroughly enjoyed learning to ride, which was a real first for me, as I had never really enjoyed driving up to that point. I passed my first motorcycle license test easily, and even though I had an accident that wrecked my first bike beyond repair, three weeks later I was back on a new bike and roaming all over the country. I passed every license test with ease and began to thoroughly enjoy every minute I spent on the road. The restriction of fear that held me captive for so long had vanished, and I was now free to experience my own independence. I have been riding ever since and still thoroughly enjoy it, and I am more than capable of driving a car these days without the powerful fear-based restriction that once gripped me so strongly.

Looking back on this experience I do not believe that any of this could have happened had I not had the cause of this restriction broken over my life through prayer. I understand that some people would have just "pushed through it and done it anyway," but for a person with a very high emotional and spiritual awareness such as myself I found this almost impossible. The problem could not be pushed to the side or overlooked; it needed to be cut off from the source. I recognize that it was a very strange thing to have a hold in my life, and it didn't make a lot of sense to me when my mother first told me about what she felt God had shown her, but I cannot deny the change that I experienced once I realized this.

This was not a one-off experience. God would reveal many more issues to me that stemmed from this area. Another thing I noticed about myself from a young age was that I seemed to have a powerful fear of either being at home or having to return home. Whenever I went away for a while I always found myself dreading the return home, as I felt so strongly that I would be in danger if I was there. This did not make sense to me rationally, as there was no real reason to fear being back at home. Our family had issues, the same as all families do, but there was nothing at home that could have created this powerful need to stay away as much as possible. It felt as if there was a little kid inside me saying,

"Please, please, I beg you. Don't send me back there. That is a bad place, and they are going to do terrible things to me and force me to do terrible things. I fear having to go back there more than anything. Please let me stay here!" Those cries were cries of total desperation and hopelessness, as though the child knew that it would not be listened to, and the more it protested the more hopeless its situation became.

This could not be solved with any change in location or situation. It continued long after I moved out of my parents' house. Whenever I was away from home—wherever that was—these same powerful feelings would come over me to the point where I sometimes extended my time away from home just so that I could delay going back there a bit longer. The fear and the despair was so powerful I would sometimes find myself holding back tears out of desperation at having to return to this place I dreaded going back to so much.

I felt so strongly that where I lived or worked was not a safe place, and those feelings remained regardless of where I was living or what job I was doing. Whenever some kind of confrontation or argument arose in either of these places, it was like my whole heart just shut down out of fear, and I would just try to make myself as small as possible and hide from the sheer terror I was feeling. These feelings tormented me for years and never seemed to improve. They contributed very strongly to my struggles with anxiety and controlling behavior, as I felt that I needed to be constantly on my guard in case something bad happened.

One day in utter desperation I cried out to God from the bottom of my heart as to what this was and why I was suffering so badly from it. God showed me that nothing had happened to me personally to have caused this but that I had inherited these powerful feelings of abuse and the dreadful fear and hopelessness that comes with it from someone generations back in the family line. Once I realized this I asked for prayer from people that I knew would understand. The prayer helped me substantially, as it broke the hold of it over my life, but I still found that there were other parts to it that I needed to process fully through talking the feelings through so that I could be totally free of it. This was not an easy thing to face, as I was also forced to realize that I had built much of my life on running away from this issue. I was also forced to realize just how much time and energy I had wasted trying to protect myself from it. However, now that I had come face to face with it I was able to start working toward becoming free of it.

Whenever these types of feelings would arise I learned to explore them and ask myself what I was feeling in regards to this. Very often I found myself asking for prayer about feelings that had no logical reason to be in my own heart yet were still very strong and needed to be cut off at the source. Often the source turned out to be the result of what I call "spiritual inheritance." The Bible mentions this in the following scripture: "Jesus replied, 'This kind can be cast out only by prayer'" (Mark 9:29, NLT). My experience with driving—and my fears regarding going home—confirmed with me just how true that scripture really was.

Learning to Handle Trials and Tribulations

Most Christians are aware of the biblical concept of strength and character being forged into a person through times of hardship and suffering. The following scripture sums it up perfectly: "Remember how the Lord your God led you all the way in the desert these forty years, to humble you and to test you in order to know what was in your heart, whether or not you would keep his commands" (Deut. 8:2–3). I found myself in some very testing times, especially during the early years of my Christian walk. Though I had read about the concept of God making people stronger and more capable through suffering, I initially did not understand how it worked and found myself despising the difficult circumstances that I was in, until I finally began to understand a way to take good things out of suffering that actually worked for me.

Being in some sort of emotional turmoil was a daily thing for me, and I would spend my days trying to manage what was within me and trying to control my external circumstances in order to keep everything within me restrained. However, this required an enormous amount of time and energy and very often left me restless yet exhausted. Once God began to test me through trials, this old mind-set went into overdrive, and rather than try to learn from the hardship I desperately fought to get myself out of it as quickly as possible.

However, nothing changed for me with regard to how I was feeling, and I began to slowly realize that the trials and tribulation I was facing were actually far less to do with my circumstances than to do with me and my own heart. I realized that by simply trying to push away the feelings that were triggered I was only doing myself a disservice. I realized that in order to actually find a way through these difficulties I needed to learn to exercise the strong sense of discernment that God was beginning to outwork within me, and that every bit of emotional turmoil I experienced was not so much a burden as an opportunity to learn something new about myself. It was a chance to build a little bit more toward the strong foundation of peace that God wanted for my life.

I began to realize that everyday situations that triggered negative emotions in my life were an opportunity for growth. For example, someone might do something that inconvenienced me, such as push in front of me in a queue, and my heart would explode into a churning turmoil of uncontrolled emotions. I could have very easily written that off as being the other person's fault for jumping in front of me and justified my own reaction to it; however, I would often find that the turmoil from situations such as this would remain long after the event had actually taken place. It was as if God were trying to tell me something along the following lines:

Even though what that person did was wrong—
and it is easy to just ignore the situation and
not think about it again—I want to show you
something with this. This happened for a
reason. Look at how you reacted. There is something buried within you that I have allowed to
be shown up through this difficulty. Do not
run from this. Do not ignore it, and do not try
and push it out of your mind—but do not lash
out at this situation in your anger. This is not
about them, but about the clarity and wholeness
I am working into you. Use the discernment I
am working into your life, and be honest with
Me about exactly what you are feeling. There is
something in your emotions that has triggered
your frustration with that person that I want
you to be free of. Examine it with Me, and we
will find the answer together, and you will move
forward and take from it what I wanted you to
learn.

The greatest revelation of truth that came to me
throughout this message was that in the depth of every
hurt and every spiritual barrier in my life there was
some sort of message or reason that was either unknown
to me or repressed. Because it was hidden it was able
to brood and fester and was able to cause pain and suffering. I slowly began to learn that identifying the message buried deep within the hurt was where the healing
would come from that I was looking for. Journeying into
the wound itself was the most painful part of the process, as the closer that I got to the root of it the more it

would hurt and the more I would want to turn and run away. But I knew I would only be doing myself a disservice if I were to run from what God was outworking within me. I found that once I could get to the root I was able to define exactly what it was that was holding this pain captive inside me. I would then tend to just blurt it out to God in prayer and in that instant, every trace of the pain from that particular wound would leave my body, and I would feel a little bit lighter inside.

For example, someone may have said something offensive to me for no reason and then disappeared before I could respond. Immediately my heart would explode into anger and rage, and I would immediately begin to pray through the emotions I was feeling with God. The prayers would often go something like this: "God, I am angry and frustrated that people can do things like that and just get away with it. It is cowardly behavior, and it is frustrating to be on the receiving end of another person's inability to deal with their own hearts! Why do I have to put up with this? I am so tired of having to put up with people's issues the same way I had to put up with that kid who pushed me around while I walked home from school when I was a kid! I felt small and powerless and frustrated at myself for not being able to do anything to stop it!" The last part was the message that held the pain captive, and all I needed to do was say that—and the pain vanished at once.

There were times when God made it very clear that there was some kind of a generational tie in the spiritual realm that was holding the pain captive and could only come out through intercessory prayer. In those cases I would need to seek out prayer from someone whom I trusted. However, I found that mostly all I needed to do was face the full extent of the hurt within me. Once I had described the message that was holding the pain captive within me to God, I would get the release I was looking for. I really took this scripture to heart: "Then you will know the truth, and the truth will set you free" (John 8:32). As I learned the truth about the pain that I was carrying I began to find the freedom I was looking for.

God gave me a vision of a man who had taken a bullet wound to the leg. However, instead of having the wound treated he had simply learned to live his life around the wound by only using one leg. God then put him in a place where he was forced to use his wounded leg, which of course brought incredible pain to the wounded man. Though having to put pressure on his wounded leg was extremely painful, it made him aware that there was a problem that needed to be resolved. Once he felt the pain he had three choices: to stop and honestly assess the wound, then take steps to heal it (keep walking on both legs, ignoring the pain screaming out at him—which would never bring him any peace and only make things worse), or start hopping around on one leg again and wait for the pain in the wounded leg to subside so that he could forget about it again.

I realized that I had one of these choices to make whenever God brought up a painful emotional wound or spiritual tie in my life. I could honestly face and assess the wound in order to heal it, continue to charge forward with the pain screaming out at me and make things worse, or try to control the situation so that the pain would settle back down within me and not bother me again. Taking the third option seemed like the right choice, but in reality it was just causing me to stagnate, as I would just get stuck on the same issues over and over again. The second choice never worked for me and only ever made me feel worse. The first choice was the choice God wanted me to take—and the true path to peace and healing.

I realized just how important it was to find the message buried deep within the pain. It was painful and uncomfortable being in that position of trying to find it, as being in that place of painful awareness but not yet being clear on what was causing it could be very distressing. However, when I asked God for insight He would always give it to me, and I knew that finding the message would truly release it from my heart. Often God would give me mental images of situations where the pain had come from. I had to be careful to try and listen to these, as it could be very easy to overlook them since they often didn't fit with what my natural mind thought the pain would truly be rooted in. At first I would ignore the thoughts when they came through. But God taught me to listen to what He was telling me in my mind and spirit in regard to where the pain was rooted, and I would find the answer there, even if it didn't make sense in my natural mind. God told me not to be afraid of being honest with Him, and that I could tell Him my darkest and ugliest secrets without fear of shame, as confessing to Him would bring release.

As I began to talk and pray through my feelings I noticed an amazing thing happen—life actually began to get easier. The more that I embraced this way of thinking, and the deeper that I went with God, the more clarity I began to find, and over time I really began to sense a strong change within myself. I would look back to where I was a year ago and realize just how far I had really come. I also began to find that circumstances would get easier and that things that would have bothered me in the past would no longer tie my stomach in knots. Instead I would have a sense of peace and clarity within myself that was never present previously.

The beginning of this journey was by far the hardest. Days of black depression were not uncommon during this emotional rollercoaster ride and very often it seemed like the moment you smashed down one brick wall and moved forward with joy, you simply ran straight into another one. What made it especially hard was the expectation of how you were supposed to function as a person now that you were considered a Christian. I felt that Christians were expected to be cheery, happy people at all times that never did anything wrong and were always so kind and loving and meek and mild. This was a hard pill to swallow for me, as I did not feel anything like that at all. I often found myself to be very moody and frustrated, and I found myself returning to old habits, which I knew were not good for me. I did not feel like a shining light at all; instead, I felt so guilty and so fake when putting up a front of happiness.

The farther that I journeyed within myself, the more I learned about myself and what was driving the perfectionism, addictive behavior, and anxiety that had dominated my entire life. It was often very ugly and throughout some of the periods when I was working very deeply with God within my own heart, highly unpredictable mood swings were not uncommon. I could go from feeling happy to hitting a major depressive slump the next moment, as something would surface in me which I had not fully come to terms with yet. That was always the hardest part—when I became consciously aware of a hurt or spiritual barrier that had previously been buried deep within my subconscious mind. Yet I was still to find the answer to what was holding it there, so until that happened it was like having the awareness of having a piece of glass stuck in your foot but not being able to do anything about it.

However, as difficult as things often were, this was an internal building process that God was working within me. God had given me the tools to think with that would help me to get through these dark places. Even though I would often crash into black moods of depression I would also find that I was doing a little better than I was the time previously and that I would learn to get through the next wall and come out of it quicker. It was a process, and more often than not it was two steps forward, one step back. However I was making progress, and I would often look back and realize that even though I was still hitting some very hard patches I had come a long way—and this was what drove me to keep going as I knew that it was worth it.

As time went on I slowly began to learn not to be afraid of facing the pain within me, as facing it and getting through it was actually helping me respond to things better and overall was improving my quality of life. It was very slow—too slow for my liking. However, I looked at this process as God building a strong foundation of peace in my life to replace the endless brokenness of before. A strong foundation needs to be very well built, with no shortcuts taken—and this is exactly what God was doing with me.

JOURNALING

Learning to find my way through the trials and difficulties I found myself facing throughout my Christian walk using the honesty I began to develop in prayer and the sense of discernment that I was developing often led me to journaling. I found that journaling would help increase my clarity on whatever I was facing within myself and also found a powerful sense of release through getting everything out in the open.

I was first introduced to this technique by a guidance counselor when I was seventeen, before I recommitted my life to Christ. I was struggling with relationships at the time and did not quite know how to handle the feelings I was experiencing. My counselor suggested that I should write a letter to people who had upset me and tell them exactly what I wanted to say without any restraint or fear and then burn the letter. They would never see what I had written, but the counselor suggested it, as he thought I might find it helpful.

I took his advice and started writing letters to people who had upset me, and although I initially found it somewhat helpful, it did not give me the full extent of the emotional release that I was looking for, so I abandoned the technique for the time being. Though it did bring some kind of release, it never really seemed to get to the core of what was really going on. I used it fervently after going through some hard times involving personal relationships, but it still felt as if I were only scratching the surface. Once I became a Christian I still kept everything within me, as I subconsciously felt that journaling would not be able to help, seeing as I felt that it had let me down before.

However, God had other ideas. One of the hardest times in my Christian walk was shortly before my twenty-second birthday, when I was not in an ideal working environment and had invested in emotional connections with people I really shouldn't have. The constant stress and frustration created an almost unbearable tension within me. I had also just been officially diagnosed with OCD, which I found extremely difficult to cope with, especially with everything else that was happening at the time. Things did not turn out well for me in this circumstance, and I found myself violently ill to the point where I needed to be hospitalized due to a stomach ulcer caused by high stress, poor eating habits, and a stomach bug. After that everything went downhill—the unhealthy emotional connections were broken, which was a good thing (but nonetheless very hard to face at the time), and I was forced to resign from my job due to my poor health. I felt as if I had lost everything and that everything within me was in constant and indefinable chaos.

One day I found myself at the computer, and I felt very strongly I should write down what I was feeling about everything. So I just started to type. I wasn't writing to anyone in particular, just trying to get a handle on what I felt was going on. I began to feel a real sense of release as I began to do this. I felt encouraged by God to delve deeply into what I was feeling and express that through journaling—instead of just writing about the circumstances, to write about the full extent of what I was feeling, without any hindrance or any holding back. This was the same as the way that God had shown me to pray at times, except instead this time I was writing it down.

I began to use this technique constantly. I could fill pages and pages of documents on the computer just detailing everything that was happening to me. Pain was brought to my attention and stayed in my face until I got the chance to sit down and pick it apart through journaling about it. It was never pleasant to read, but once again it was honest, and that was the most important thing. God then showed me why journaling originally did not work for me when I was younger.

When I was seventeen I approached journaling in a very selfish way, simply trying to blame the other person and fire all of my frustration at them for what was happening to me emotionally. God showed me that this technique was shallow and selfish and that I would not find the release that I was looking for through passing the blame. That was why it wasn't working for me. Instead I learned that I had to fully express, pick apart, and dissect the depth of the emotions within me if I wanted to be free; that was where journaling came in. But I couldn't do it in a self-pitying sort of way or through trying to blame others. Instead I had to take a stark, brutal, and honest look at myself and using the discernment and honesty that I was developing, to write everything down. This is an example of one of my journals I wrote regarding the victim mentality. I have shown it exactly as I wrote it, without editing it:

> People would look at me with the knowledge that they could treat me as badly as they liked and that they would be able to get away with it. People were free to express the full rottenness of the evil in their hearts toward me and dump it all on me without any fear of repercussion and were free to take me for granted and mistreat me as much as they wanted and exercise every part of their free will against me because they needed to have an outlet to abuse and mistreat and vandalize and disrespect and mutate where they could use all of their cowardly weaponry against me without any fear of repercussion because they had been abused as well and

the abusive mentality lies to people and tells them that the way out of their problems is to abuse someone weaker than you and it provides a false sense of freedom but it is a lie and only adds to the cycle and makes things worse for everyone. I have adopted this mentality myself and I expressed my own frustration against my friends and abused them and picked on them while ignoring their needs until some of them were too afraid to go to school. Abusing those weaker than you is pathetic and cowardly and I have done this very thing myself. Standing up to someone who you know controls you and you know that you have to submit to and are afraid of is the worst thing you can ever do because all you ever get back is a cruel and belittling response which is based on the fact that they know that you are afraid of them because they can sense it. I cannot fight someone I am afraid of as my fear controls me and makes me desperately vulnerable. I know that I am afraid of them and that fear poisons every part of my being and they know that because I am afraid of them I am no threat to them for people have used fear to control me and have installed fear in my life and used my own fear as a tool to control me which covers over me like a blanket and makes sure that I cannot move without some sort of fear based handle connected to my heart being used to control me. People know that it is there and I know that it is there and I know that because I am afraid of them I can never overcome them and I cannot win and as usual I am defeated by my own fear. My own fear tells me that I can never overcome anything and that I am too weak and that the moment I try to give the illusion of strength I will be found out for being weak and spineless and therefore rubbished and ridiculed for being a liar as I am lying about my strength. Those who abuse me know my fear and know how weak I am so they know that they can get away with it.

This process was ugly, and the journals themselves were raw and often violent in content. However, they were honest, and God was using this honest form of writing to help further develop my discernment as to what was happening within me. He was doing that in order to bring a stronger sense of emotional articulation and therefore peace and clarity through understanding. I was learning to effectively use a technique that would greatly benefit me for years to come.

LEARNING ABOUT RESPONSIBILITIES

I knew little of true personal responsibilities when I first became a Christian, and I was strongly affected by the worldly mind-set that "nothing's ever my fault; everyone else is responsible, not me." Occasionally that mind-set would work in reverse, and I would find myself feeling responsible for everything, depending on the situation. However, this was not right either, and it was not uncommon for me to swing from one extreme to the other.

I mentioned previously that I was often the subject of bullying throughout my childhood and teenage years. People would pick on me, as they could sense that I was not a strong person and not able to defend myself, so they perceived that they could get away with what they did, which of course was very wrong and was an outworking of sin in their lives. Being treated in this manner created a furious anger and frustration within me, yet when I had the opportunity to confront anyone who treated me in this way, more often than not I would shrink back in fear rather than stand up for myself, as I felt powerless and unable to stop them from hurting me—even if I tried.

I felt very angry that I was treated this way to begin with, and I also felt a lot of anger toward myself for being too weak to fight back. I would lump all of the responsibility for any situations where I felt I was bullied onto the other parties involved and would take none for myself. I didn't think I needed to as, after all, they were the ones bullying me. I harbored a powerful sense of self-righteousness and injustice. I felt as if I had not done anything wrong, and no one could convince me otherwise. Although I was justified in feeling angry at those who mistreated me, it was only part of the story.

God revealed to me that I was harboring a lot of fear in my life that would subtly influence me to bow down and let other people abuse and push me around. Though the people who treated me abusively were (and are) responsible for their own actions in the eyes of God, the people that bullied me in my life were not responsible for me sitting back and allowing them to do it and not standing up and being strong. I was responsible for this, as I had allowed this to happen through embracing fear and living out of it. It was so easy for me to find excuses: "I didn't know what I was doing when I embraced that. It was too subtle. I didn't notice I was doing it. Woe is me," and so on and so on. I could easily have tried to sulk and have a pity party—and could undoubtedly have found many reasons to do so. However, God showed me that even though others were in the wrong, I was still responsible for my own feelings. I was unable to find release in deferring my own responsibilities onto other people or trying to make excuses for myself and my fearful behavior. I also realized that God would not blame me for harboring fear. He would simply show me that even though I may have embraced it at a young age without realizing it, it still needed to be removed from my life. I did not feel condemned by God throughout all this, He was simply telling me that regardless of how any of this fear made it into my heart I was still responsible for getting rid of it.

This was a messy process, especially to begin with. If someone wronged me and I could not escape from what I was feeling, I would very easily lash out at the person whom I felt had wronged me in my own mind. However, as God was trying to teach me, lashing out at them was not the answer and would often only make me feel worse. There were times when I was a lot younger when I actually took physical revenge on people who had wronged me. But, in fact, I found that I hurt myself through doing it far more than I did them. I knew subconsciously that taking revenge was not going to solve anything in my own heart. As I got older I did not tend to act out in this way, but the desire was still there. There would usually be a bit of raging in frustration to God about what they had done in my own mind until I remembered that this also wouldn't solve anything and that the answer to solving this was to ask God what was really happening in my own heart.

As I slowly learned to embrace this truth, I discovered an amazing thing: the more I began to own up to and face my own responsibilities in situations, I would find the release that I was looking for. Trying to place *all* of the blame at the feet of others was not helping me at all. Of course, there were times when God made it clear to me in that the other parties involved were fully responsible for the situation and that I had no actions I needed to repent of in His eyes. But all too often I began to see just how I would try and defer my own responsibilities onto other people, which would never bring me any release. As I embraced this truth over time and learned to ask myself and God what parts of any situations that had arisen were *my* responsibilities I began to find a peace and release I had never truly experienced previously.

There was also another side to this issue. I would often take responsibility for things that I was not actually responsible for. God showed me that I had a problem with being responsible. This would translate in one of two ways. The way it most often worked through me was when I was wronged by others. It would immediately tell me that it was my fault that they wronged me and that they were responsible for nothing, and I was responsible for everything, so I needed to apologize to them for making them wrong me. This created a powerful sense of injustice in my life, as I felt that the wrong that was done to me automatically meant nothing; however, the stronghold of irresponsibility would not back down, so I had no choice but to do what I felt I had to do.

The other way it would translate was when I wronged someone else. It would often work through me against others in the sense that I would tell people that they deserved the abuse that I gave them and that it was their fault for making me do it, so I expected an apology from them. I was inflicting the same suffering upon other people that I had experienced myself. It could have been very easy to overlook these emotional driving forces, but God wanted to show me that there was more to it than meets the eye. This stronghold was hurting other people as well as myself, so I am thankful that God helped me to understand what was really going on so that I could bring it into His light and be free of it.

LEARNING TO UNDERSTAND
MY OWN EMOTIONS

I have heard the comment made that with some men the only two emotions they seem to express are anger and lust. I have certainly been in that position myself, and I have learned since then that emotions are far more complex than this and therefore cannot be lumped into two categories. However, for people not familiar with their own emotions or people with a lack of discernment it is easy for emotions to only translate through these two outlets.

As I began to learn about my own anger and the fear that restricted it, I also began to learn about just how complex the anger really was and how a situation that incites anger can end up becoming a vehicle to express other emotions, which can be totally unrelated. Bottling up my emotions and stuffing them away seemed like the best way to go about things, but it was really only ignoring the problem. I could eventually get to a point where I had stuffed it down so much I wouldn't have to face it. However, even though it was out of my conscious mind, the wounding in my heart remained, and it was just a matter of time before it came up again.

A huge aspect of my journey has been about emotional memory. It is so easy to feel hurt and angry by someone who has offended us. We are very often overcome with emotions and feel they are completely responsible for everything we are feeling. However, this is not always the case. When things happen to us throughout our lives, especially traumatic experiences that hurt us deeply, although we may eventually forget them in our conscious minds our emotions remember the event often in its entirety. I cringe whenever I hear those sayings "Time is the greatest healer" and "Your emotions will recover." Though these two quotes are definitely true to a certain degree, my concern is that people will grasp on to them with both hands and think that all they need to do with situations that have damaged them is forget them and all will be fixed, which I do not believe to be true.

The results surprised me. More often than not, my reactions were because of previous circumstances and not what I was currently facing. As I began to do this I began to realize just how much I had stored up over the years. I would feel the full extent of everything that had happened to me in the past like it was happening right there and then—which was a very painful experience. However, it was necessary in order to bring everything into the light so that I would be made aware of absolutely everything and not leave any emotional dregs left over. There was often a lot more to it than just simply anger. There would almost always be other emotions at play, such as fears and insecurities, for example. Usually these other factors would all just be subconsciously lumped into the anger I was feeling at any current situation, thus causing other emotions to translate simply as anger. This put more emphasis on the situation that had triggered these emotions than was actually warranted.

One of the greatest fears in my life was the fear of having to face the anger of other people—especially when I felt that they had a justified reason to be angry at me. As a result I would do everything in my power to avoid it. I eventually realized that the reason I was so highly affected by the anger of others was mainly because it would trigger the powerful, destructive anger I already held within myself. But instead of being able to use the anger as a weapon for my own benefit, when it came from a person that I did not want to be angry at me, my own anger would work in reverse and turn against me. I felt as if the fear was because of the other person and what they could do to me, when actually it was really my own feelings working against me.

One of the strongest barriers toward learning to express anger in a clear-headed and healthy manner was connected with my childhood. When I lost my temper as a child my anger was explosive and could easily translate into verbal (and often physical) abuse toward others. However I was never taken seriously. Since I was a child with a relatively small frame, all my anger would ever do was make me into a laughing stock. It seemed to me that the angrier I got, the more people laughed at me. God revealed to me that this made me feel incredibly ashamed of my own emotions and that my anger was completely incapable of changing anything around me. I began to realize that I felt like people were always going to be bigger than me and just laugh at me or punish me in order to push my anger back down into myself, because it was a joke to them. Even as an adult I still carried this mentality within me.

Another powerful truth I learned about was how easy it was to project my own emotions onto outward circumstances and blame people for my own feelings. Probably the easiest example to use for this is road rage. Often when I was on my motorcycle, other drivers would do stupid things, such as pull out right in front of me, which could have put my life in danger. My heart would explode with violent emotions, and I would very often make rude signs and gestures at the person driving the other car. In some cases I had to restrain myself from following the car in question and initiating a confrontation. In my own mind it was easy for me to just label them as a "useless driver who hates bikes," and I would very often do that and convince myself that it was true, because as far as I was concerned I had the evidence to back it up.

However, this entire theory was based on assumption. In reality, the person driving the car may have been a perfectly nice person with no malicious intent and that could have been their first mistake out of their whole driving career. However, I had just gone and labeled them as something that they were not, because my perception of the situation was not based in fact but on my own emotional interpretation. I would find it easy to project my own frustrations and emotions onto other people in this manner when I really didn't have any right to. Commenting on how they were driving was fair enough, but going overboard with personal attacks and accusations was really going by assumption rather than fact. Trying to make other people responsible for my overreaction to their driving did not help anyone, least of all me.

I began to see the frustration that I held toward others who had supposedly wronged me differently, especially when it came from people who had acted in an emotional way toward me, such as anger or frustration. Through examining my own heart and asking God for insight, He showed me that my rage toward them was actually more rage toward myself and my own circumstances for not feeling like I was free enough to act in the way that they were. I was seeing someone else act in a way that I wanted to act but I was unable to do so. My rage and frustration came from how I was imagining that I would be feeling if I were trying to act the way that they were acting toward me. I felt that if I were trying to act the way that they were I would feel a powerful sense of restriction and fear trying with all of its might to hold me back, and I felt extremely frustrated at this. I also felt furious at them for not being as restricted and controlled as I was, and I felt furious at myself for being in this position of such extreme restriction and conflict. This insight helped me to heal myself in a big way, as just admitting it took a huge amount of pressure off me.

Using these new ideas and perceptions I began to discern what was happening within me and analyze my own emotions with the help of God. I began to see more clearly in situations that would have previously affected me quite badly and I finally began to learn to separate fact from assumptions and projections based on my own emotional issues. Learning these truths helped me to learn to be more calm in situations, as I found that the more I got to know about myself and my own emotions, the better equipped I was to deal with what life threw at me and the more accurately I would be able to interpret different situations.

THE COMPLEXITY OF MENTAL ILLNESS AND THE CHRISTIAN FAITH

Being a Christian is not an easy process to begin with, but being a Christian whilst struggling with a mental illness is a totally different matter altogether. I began to utilize the techniques I have outlined in this book, but due to the strong sense of perception I had, and coupled with the anxiety I experienced on a daily basis, facing the pain and the darkness could be a very complicated and sometimes incredibly confusing and frustrating process. If the pain I was trying to face was rooted in some kind of message that I was overlooking or felt that I was unable to discern, it would not go away. Then I would be trying very hard to describe the pain in order to reveal the message that held it captive—but feeling as if I was getting nowhere. Sometimes it very much felt as if I was using the approach of "throw a whole lot of mud at the wall and see if something sticks" in order to find the answer I was looking for.

This is where I had to remind myself to continually ask God for guidance and clarity as to what I was struggling with, as His Holy Spirit would give me the insight to discern the message that held the pain captive. I just had to remember to ask Him for it. In the deepest and darkest places of confusion I would often feel God saying to me, "You can do it, Graham. The message is there. You are so close! You can put it into words and free yourself. I know you can." Though it was hard, and could be very alienating toward those around me, as I often seemed overly silent and uncommunicative, this was the foundation to getting well.

Now I believe there was definitely a chemical imbalance in my brain, which contributed greatly to the anxiety I struggled with, and this was heightened by using marijuana in my teenage years. But most of what fueled the anxiety and fear-based behavior in my life had far more to do with my own emotional strongholds and negative spiritual inheritance than it did a chemical imbalance. The emotional and spiritual strongholds that held my soul captive were very deeply rooted and therefore often very difficult to accurately define. The deeply held pain and anguish of these issues would underscore nearly everything that I did and said and gave rise to the behavior of obsession and anxiety associated with mental illness.

These deeply rooted hurts and spiritual strongholds certainly infected my Christian faith and my walk with God. For example, I would often feel tormented into going to someone to apologize for something by an urging in my emotions justifying the demands, saying that "this is what God wants you to do." So, thinking I was being obedient, I would go and do it. Someone may have treated me in a manner that I did not deserve to be treated. Instead of accurately realizing that this issue was their problem, I would feel tormented into going to that person to apologize to them for making them mistreat me in the first place. This was, of course, the outworking of some of the spiritual strongholds I carried within myself. However, I would think that it was God and would therefore do as I thought He had told me and would make myself look like even more of a victim in the process.

I found it incredibly difficult to try to receive good things from God due to these issues. I was constantly told that God was gracious, loving, and forgiving; that I had nothing to fear; and that my life was headed for awesome things. However, I found this almost impossible to receive and believe due to the deeply rooted issues of pride, victimization, and fear in my life. Fear of receiving was a huge part of my struggles. I honestly believed that there was nothing outside of my own heart other than evil and that if I opened my heart to receive anything from anyone all I would receive was abuse, violence, and control based in fear and negativity. My response to this was to become completely self-reliant and to refuse to give anyone anything that they could ever use against me, which also contributed to my fear of anger. I believed the only person in the world I could ever rely on was myself. Having any kind of faith that actually depended on God was incredibly difficult as a result of this issue.

Many Christian people offered to counsel me and try to help me through my problems over the years. Though this did help, I managed to alienate many of the people who offered counsel to me over the years, as it just didn't seem to be getting anywhere. I would talk myself ragged and go into great detail describing what was happening within me, yet I would also feel that people were becoming more and more tired of my endless rambling.

I believe this is because the full extent of the messages that were holding the pain captive in my life was being overlooked somehow on my part, and I was just "chopping the branches off the tree," so to speak, instead of uprooting it altogether. There was a limit to the extent that people could help me, and I believe that my emotional problems were so deeply rooted that I was almost beyond the help of people around me. Hence the reason many relationships with counselors often appeared to grow more and more strained over time.

God's response to all of this was to discipline me in a loving manner in order to show me these strongholds that kept me from truly connecting with Him along with continuing to give me the insight I needed to overcome my struggles. I remember crying out to God one day in prayer with the words, "I don't need discipline; I need love." God's response—that still, small voice in my heart—caught me off guard: "You need discipline so that you can receive My love." I could easily have found excuses to remain the way that I was and could easily have resigned my life to being controlled by my internal issues. I was once offered to leave work and go on a sickness benefit due to my mental health struggles, but I chose to keep going forward, to keep listening to God, and to keep on fighting these issues.

Hope in the Darkness

Throughout everything I was learning to break through, there was one essential factor to the whole process that

I became more and more aware of over time: the great love and endless patience that God has for people, especially those who struggle with any form of mental illness.

There were many times when I wanted to give up on the whole journey and just go back to an easy life swayed by the overpowering emotions I struggled with, using substances and distractions to medicate my feelings. But as much as I wanted to give up, God never, ever gave up on me. The deep work of healing and surfacing wounded emotions and spiritual strongholds was incredibly painful; however, I also realized that God's work in bringing this to the surface was not out of some heartless desire to make me perfect but simply because God loved me enough to want to restore me fully, even down to the darkest and most broken parts of my own soul.

Imagine God is a great lover of old cars, and I am a rusty, broken-down wreck, slowly rotting from the inside out. Instead of being repulsed by the rotting wreck He sees before Him, He sees that rusty, broken old car and is filled with love and compassion and wants to restore that car to full working order. So He takes it home, shuts it in His garage, and begins the rebuilding process. It is very slow and thorough, because He wants to take as much time as He needs in order to get everything just right. Rust is removed; moving parts are either restored or sometimes replaced altogether. The engine is completely rebuilt from the ground up and all of the rust and dirt is thoroughly cleaned out.

After much time and much hard work, the car is now finished and fully restored. The car entered the garage a dirty, repulsive wreck but emerges as a gleaming example of how something that was once broken could be completely restored with love, patience and hard work. The owner is now very proud of what He has done and wants to show the world what He has done with this old wreck. He beams with pride as He drives it through the city and shows His friends what He has done with it. He is proud to call it His own.

I certainly felt the pain of having the rust scoured out of my life. I wanted nothing more than to just turn and run somewhere where it could not hurt anymore. It hurt very much when I had to stand in that place of pain and face it rather than run away from it. It was often easy to forget that this was something done out of love, as it certainly didn't feel very loving at the time. But true love—or love based in truth—can hurt. Pain can be productive, and the pain of having the darkness scoured out of my life was far better than the numbness that you get from medicating issues rather than facing them.

One of the first revelations I remember receiving as a new Christian was that God actually understood what was happening to me. Throughout life I often felt as if I were either ridiculed and mocked for the way that I was or disciplined heavily. Reaching out to others became nearly impossible, as I felt that those were the only two responses I would receive. However, it was not the same with God. I felt very much that He was looking down upon me and saying to me, "I understand why you are the way that you are in a way that nobody else ever could. I can help you, not in a superficial way, but in a way that will build the peace into your life that you have been craving as long as you have been alive. You can tell Me anything. I know everything about you anyway. Even your darkest and ugliest secret has always been known to Me, and I have paid the price for it on the cross. The only part that is left is the outworking of this in your life, which will break these bondages. This will be dark, and it will be painful, but it is your true path to healing. I will never give up on you."

Finding a place of true understanding for my struggles was ultimately the foundation I have built my relationship with God upon. Never once did I feel like I was being treated with disdain, and never once did I feel like God had turned against me, despite the depth of the ugliness He was bringing up out of my heart. To this day, there is only one place I ever feel truly safe and truly free to express whatever I need to, and that is in prayer with the God who will not give up on me no matter what and will not stop until His work in me is complete.

I remember one particular year where I was facing some very difficult circumstances, and the pain I was trying to face seemed to be endless. I began to get very discouraged and even began to doubt that I was doing the right thing. Some good friends gathered around me and prayed for me one night. I will never forget the words one of them spoke over me: "Keep going, for you've made progress. It might feel like two steps forward and one step back, but you have made progress. I see you throwing off the shackles and laughing as you are doing it. The key to your struggles is inside of you—nowhere else." That word encouraged me so much to keep facing the pain in this manner and led me to believe that despite how hard it was—and how consumed by darkness I often felt—this was the path that God wanted me to walk.

Learning to Break the Cycle of Injustice

The cycle of frustration, confusion, and anger caused by some sort of perceived injustice was one I found myself in many times throughout the years. When I felt that I was in a place where I could express anger at a circumstance I believed was unfair without fear of retribution that hardened attitude would often fester and come through to the surface, and I would often take it out on the person in question, even if they had nothing to do with it. Often, the other person would then react toward me with anger for how I was treating them, and this is where the dangerous cycle began. I would subconsciously think along the following lines:

> That person back then really hurt me and upset me, and now this person has become angry at me too. It's not fair. I'm not the one in the wrong. That person back then should never have done this in the first place, and then I wouldn't be angry. I should be able to lash out at this person now, as they owe me something—or are supposed to care about me. And they should understand, but instead they are rebuking me. They don't care about me at all—only the way that

I act. They just want me to be good regardless
of how much I am upset over what happened.
They are just as uncaring as the person who
hurt me to begin with, only in a different way!

This would then cause me to become bitter and defensive toward the current situation, and the cycle would continue. The more I tried to get out, the worse it got. It was almost like being at the bottom of a hole, and I felt as if I could dig my way out. Instead, I was only ever digging myself in deeper. The frustration of realizing that I was making things worse would simply fuel me to make things worse yet again. I damaged many relationships this way throughout the years, some irreparably. This would happen to me time and time again throughout my life, and each time I wouldn't learn a thing; I would only ever become even more bitter and twisted than before. That, in turn, fueled the inevitable destruction of future relationships with others. This would then bring injustice upon them, as they were treated unfairly due to my own anger. If I was to be confronted, rather than take any responsibility I would look to the source of what caused me to be angry in the first place and place all of the blame on that, rather than take responsibility for how I was acting and realize that my behavior was hurting others.

Eventually, with the help of God, I began to learn the truth. I realized that I was often holding onto truth in this situation, which was why I grasped it so tightly. However, it was only part of the truth. There was often more to why the original situation even happened than what I was choosing to remember. I think that even back then, deep down I was subconsciously aware of the full extent of the truth, yet because it didn't fit into things the way that I wanted it to, I ignored the truth and made things even worse for myself. This confusion and conflict created a huge amount of frustration, which would spill over into situations. When I thought that people were being awful to me and telling me that I was not allowed to be myself, all that was actually happening was that they were putting up boundaries to protect themselves from me, which was fair enough. However, being already deeply embedded in a state of confusion and conflicted frustration, I would believe the lie that they were just out to get me like everyone else and would become enraged and bitter toward them.

I realized that trying to solve my complex internal problems by using them as a weapon to try to make other people back down was never going to solve any-thing. I was so certain in my own mind that "if this person would just apologize or admit defeat, then I would finally be happy and be released from this and feel better." This mentality would cause me to either utilize threat-ening behavior toward others to try and force them into backing down so that I would feel better or, if it trans-lated internally, would cause me to hold grudges and powerful resentments for long periods of time. However, neither of these two techniques ever worked, especially not the first one. Most of the time people whom I tried to overpower with intimidation would not tolerate my behavior and would respond accordingly, which would send me into a fit of rage. The first level of anger hadn't worked, so I felt as if I had to take it up a notch.

However, these actions only ever seemed to create a fight-fire-with-fire type response, which could easily have ended up in someone getting hurt and nothing ever getting resolved—and the cycle of injustice would continue, with two people forever trying to one-up the other one. It was a vicious and pathetic cycle, and it made me feel incredibly weak and helpless, as I believed for the longest time that my problems with people in this manner could only be resolved through aggression, and the more others fought back against me, the weaker I felt. I was forced to realize that trying to use intimidation or grudges toward other people to get them to do what I wanted would not solve anything in my own heart, and it was just a matter of time before the entire process of trying to one-up people started again with someone else. I actually also found that the more anger and frustration I tried to use to overpower others and the more I reacted to what people had done, the worse I would feel, as I was getting farther and farther away from getting any issues resolved, as well as adding to the powerful injustice already so present in the world today.

I learned that hanging on to the self-righteous mindset that I had every right to be bitter because someone else had wronged me was not making things any better for me. Even if they had wronged me and I had done nothing to deserve it, embracing bitterness and hatred was doing nothing but damaging the relationships I had with others. The problem may have started from someone else, but through neglecting my own responsibilities I was the one adding fuel to it. I had to learn to defuse situations by not taking the bait that was given to me to try and overpower someone else. I began to realize that if someone was trying to use threatening behavior to get me to back down it really was their problem that was eating them up from the inside and not mine. Release for me was never going to come through overpowering others. The most that it would bring was some kind of temporary satisfaction that would not last long, and that if I gave my life over fully to this I would have ended up a bitter, twisted, and angry old man with a life destined to end in failure and regret. I knew that this could have been my future, and this was not a future that I wanted.

I learned that if I was going to find peace I needed to learn to respect the boundaries of others, and I learned how to vent to people and not at people, which are two completely different things. Holding on to a small part of truth—and ignoring the rest of the picture—was setting me up for destruction. I learned to take the blinders off and to see situations from different perspectives. As I began to learn the truth, I began to break this vicious cycle through honesty and humility. I was led by God many times to humble myself and apologize to those whom I felt had wronged me or had stood up to me for acting inappropriately. Perhaps they were not completely in the right either, that's true, but God led me to apologize for what was my part in the situation. Eventually I began to learn that the actions of others were not my responsibility and that my responsibility was for my own heart and actions, not the heart or actions of anyone else.

LEARNING TO BREAK THE CYCLE OF ABUSE

Abuse in my life was another cycle I needed to break. Because of the abuse I had received throughout my life through bullying, I often felt as if I gained some sort of emotional release out of bullying other people. Throughout the times when I was being abused and too fearful to stand up to it I was translating the frustration from that onto other people. I was feeding the cycle through my own dishonesty. I was giving the abuser the power to continue to abuse and mistreat me through harboring the fear in my own heart. Although the other parties in question were responsible for their own behavior, I was responsible for allowing it to continue and continuing the cycle. I had the power to break the cycle, although I didn't realize it yet.

I believed thoroughly that I had no power and that I could not stop the bullying, because I believed that the bullying party was in control. However, I eventually began to realize that I was actually allowing them to run riot through my fear. Rather than face the fears head on and deal with them, which would break the cycle, I would try and find another outlet for my emotions, such as a weaker person. As long as I refused to deal with the fear that subconsciously gave bullies the license to treat me badly, they had nothing to worry about. I was the one allowing this to happen—and it was only me who had the power to stop it.

Facing my fears in this regard was a terrifying and painful process; however, I needed to face and deal with the full extent of the fear if I was to ever hope to get out of this cycle. I could not rely on someone else to change, as there would always be someone else out there who would try to take advantage of me. As long as I continued to rely on other people not to treat me badly I was only ever going to be reinforcing the victim mentality over my life. I was already in control of the situation without realizing it through what I allowed people to do to me out of fear. I simply needed to deal with the fear that allowed them to have power over me and then stand firm against them once it had been dealt with. Simply trying to confront people who were mistreating me while shaking in my boots may have rectified the situation in question, but it was not changing the powerful strongholds in my heart that made me a victim to begin with.

As I learned to heal and learned to face my fears I began to realize that what I feared so much in people that I perceived as bullies actually had very little to do with the subject in question. I had projected the sense of my own fears onto them, and I felt by bowing down to the person in question I could soothe the fear and anxiety within my own soul. As I began to free myself of the fears, I began to find that I felt far less vulnerable to the very people I was once terrified of. Now I began to see them in a more accurate light, which was not clouded by my own fears and perceptions. I found that as I healed more and became stronger, the subconscious vibes I gave off began to slowly change from the fearful vibe of a victim to a vibe of someone who carried himself with confidence and therefore deserved respect. The only way that bullies were truly able to control me was through the fear that gripped my own heart, and once that fear began to dissipate, they no longer had anything they could control me with. The cycle of abuse began to break and inner healing began to destroy the victim mentality that had ruled my life.

Eventually I began to learn that I believed that I was too weak to be able to fight back and that I was worthless, so I would react passively and let people abuse me because a message deeply imprinted in my heart would say, "I am weak. I am powerless without you. You treat me badly, but I feel as if I have no choice but to please you, because I have nowhere else to go. No one else would ever take me in and understand if I left you. I do not believe in myself, and you are treating me badly, so you must believe in yourself. I want to be like you. This is why I will stay around." This deeply imprinted, fear-based message would consistently show in my behavior and would make me an easy target for people to pick on. I could not break this fear off my life through just trying to push through it with strength, as that would have become overwhelming. I realized that trying to just force my way through it without truly facing it felt like trying to run with an elastic band attached to me that would get tighter and pull me back harder the more that I ran. I could not break through this fear in this manner. It had to be cut off at the source.

I realized too that I that actually I felt as if I deserved the abuse I had received. I have always struggled with a powerful sense of self-judgment and a very high level of self-criticism. I would always feel that things were somehow my fault and that I deserved what people were saying or doing to me, so for me the punishment was deserved. Anything I tried to do to stand up to those abusing me would result in worse treatment. If I were to stand and fight back I would be wrong on two levels—for doing something to initiate the abuse in the first place and then trying to defend myself for it later on. I believed this, and it held a powerful influence over my life.

This would go the other way as well. I would show critical and belittling attitudes toward others when I felt I was able to get away with it. Whenever I faced any sort of justified criticism from other people, even if it wasn't personal, I would feel incredibly condemned and judged, and either I would plunge into a dark hole of depression or into a violent external reaction. Neither of these were helpful to anyone around me and were just making the cycle worse.

When someone is abused by another person or has a victim mentality imprinted on their life from birth like I did, it is like that person has marionette strings that hold that person's heart and emotions. All that another person needs to do is see those strings holding the person's heart and take hold of them, and they are at once able to make that person their slave.

God journeyed with me deeply to break this fear-based control from my heart. Like everything, breaking this cycle was a process. I would break through one fear, but I would often find myself in a deeply fearful and vulnerable position again shortly afterward. I learned not to fear this, as I realized that I was not going backward but rather going deeper. I had broken through one layer, and now I was facing the next layer, which I needed to break through as well. It was easy to feel discouraged and feel like I was getting nowhere, but God would encourage me and would often reveal to me through circumstances just how far I had truly come by bringing me into a place where I would previously have felt a strong sense of fear. Now instead of those feelings I would feel a sense of strength I had not felt before. So, even though I was still hitting fearful places, I learned that it was God simply moving me forward into a greater place of strength. The fear I was facing was just another obstacle that would be broken down and would become a place of peace.

I also had to face up to the deep damage I had done to myself by bullying others. I realized that when I abused someone else by bullying them I was sinning in the eyes of God, and that sin would begin to weigh heavily on my conscience. I also felt powerful anger and frustration toward the fact that I was not making any progress of setting myself free and was instead abusing someone else. The more I sinned and hurt myself and my own conscience by sinning, the more ammunition

I would have to make someone else's life a living hell. I repented deeply for this behavior, as I was now beginning to become aware of the deep destruction I was leaving behind me when I abused others and ignored the consequences.

As I started to become free of the darkness that bound my heart and kept me in a place of vulnerability, I began to see my victims in a different light. Whereas previously I would subconsciously see them as a dumping ground for my own frustrations, I began to see them in a more respectful manner, and even though I may have had the opportunity to dump on them, I began to choose not to out of a place of respect for them as an individual despite the fear they carried within them. I began to have a sense of compassion and understanding for those with hearts gripped by fear and anxiety, just as mine was, and out of my experience in this area came a real desire to help people and see people set free.

LEARNING TO FORGIVE

This had always been a very complex and frustrating subject for me. It took me many years before I was truly able to understand the concept of forgiveness. Due to the victim mentality I battled with I often found myself furiously angry at people who had mistreated me for taking advantage of me, but there was also a lot of anger toward myself for letting people walk all over me and for giving fear the room to control my life and my actions.

In this state of highly complicated emotional confusion, being told that I had to forgive those who had wronged me would often generate a negative and sometimes hostile response from me toward anyone who said that this was what I needed to do. Being told that God would not forgive me until I chose to forgive others was something I also found highly offensive, as it simply added to the already deep-seated frustration I struggled with. I would become frustrated to hear people talking about how forgiveness was something that needed to happen immediately and how you "were not doing it right" if you didn't feel 100 percent free after you had chosen to forgive another person and that God's judgment was now upon you. I tried very hard to do this, but the anger and frustration remained, and the inevitable sense that I was being judged by God for my supposed failure to forgive remained also. I felt very much that when I had been wronged, I had been deliberately victimized by people, and being told to forgive them felt like I had to go and offer myself to them for further humiliation and abuse. This was my problem and nothing to do with the person I felt had offended me. However, it still made the process of forgiveness very difficult.

I faced many offenses throughout the years, and each time these would happen I would feel that familiar sense of anger and frustration toward both them and myself. This was inevitably followed by imagined condemnation and judgment from God for not living up to what He wanted from me. This way of thinking kept me in a place of bitterness for a very long time. It was something that

I would try to avoid or overlook, but it was just a matter of time until I would have to face it again. Though I believed everything I was feeling to be true and accurate, this was not helping me at all but hurting me, and certainly was not helping me move toward a place of true forgiveness. Radical change was needed.

As time passed I began to learn to see things differently, mainly thanks to more mature people who had walked a similar path to what I was journeying through and were able to shed some light on what was a very touchy subject for me. I began to see that forgiveness is a choice based on a decision, and you cannot be expected to radically shift all negative emotions connected to the experience when you feel you have been wronged. I believe that although forgiveness is a decision, working it out is a process that involves the full acknowledgment of whatever feelings may be attached to that situation. Forgiveness does not magically make any negative emotions automatically dissipate; these need to be worked through in full and are part of the process. I learned that it is OK not to like the person that has hurt you and that boundaries do need to be set in place unless the wrong is acknowledged and repentance comes on their part.

I also learned that a lot of the fuel toward the anger and hatred toward those who had supposedly wronged me was not actually associated with them at all. Though the person had hurt me and had no doubt done wrong, I needed to forgive them for that wrong. Part of the process of working through this often meant I came to a place of realization that what had surfaced was from previous matters left unresolved. God would sometimes show me that what I was feeling was actually because of some kind of powerful spiritual stronghold in my life that needed to be dealt with through prayer. I would often realize that the person who had brought this to light by supposedly hurting me had actually done me far more of a favor than a disservice, as they had made me aware of something that needed to change from within my own heart.

I realized that when God was asking me to forgive others He was not interested in what they had done but rather my response to it. He wanted me to respond in the right way so that I would not be in the wrong as well through acting out of revenge, which would only ever make things worse. This was frustrating, as revenge seemed to be an easy outlet. However, it would not fix the problem that was within my own heart and instead led to a revenge/offence cycle that would never end. All anyone is really doing through taking revenge is trying to run from their own pain, and the more you try and run the more it ends up hurting the person taking revenge in the first place. Until the problem within their own heart is solved, it will just continue to hurt.

To paint a picture of this truth, imagine that someone feels weak and insecure within themselves. To try and take these feelings away they feel the need to go and overpower another person. If that person fights back, then the person who initiated the confrontation is now in a place where their method to try and make them feel good about themselves has been threatened by another person. The simple answer then is to take control of the situation through taking control of that person by using aggression or intimidation. Though the person in the position of power may win the argument through doing this, all that they are truly doing is using an external situation to force their insecure feelings back within themselves.

I have been in this situation before, and I know from my experience that the more I yelled at someone else to try and get them to back down, the worse I felt. I knew I was going the wrong way about the problem, and the worse I felt, the more I yelled. Even if the person I was yelling at did back down, it would only be a temporary satisfaction achieved through abusing another person. Revenge was never going to work. The problem needed to be solved through facing the feelings and working through them.

Though this was true I still felt incredibly frustrated that I had to analyze my own emotions and work through things that I felt very often had been brought upon me by other people. I always believed that revenge was the only way out, and I saw others doing it around me constantly in order to try and find some kind of personal satisfaction, even though it did not solve anything in the long run. I felt angry that I had to change my belief structures and walk a different path. I often found myself thinking, "If I have to work through this, then the person who put me in the position of making me have to work through this via their own actions should have to go through this as well. Then none of this would have happened in the first place! Why isn't God disciplining them?"

However, God is a just God—something I initially found difficult to grasp because of the injustice I had seen over the years both from others and myself. I realized that being in a place of discipline from God, being forced to face myself and analyze my emotions through the wrongs of another person, was actually a better place to be than I realized. I was gaining an awareness, which, to my mind, was badly needed by those who had supposedly wronged me in the first place. The following scriptures gave me a sense of comfort:

> My son, do not despise the LORD's discipline and do not resent his rebuke, because the LORD disciplines those he loves.
>
> —PROVERBS 3:11–12

> He punishes everyone he accepts as a son.
>
> —HEBREWS 12:6

I realized that although it was painful, it was far better to be placed in a hard place by God and to be finding answers than to be one who puts others in a hard place through their own refusal to seek out true answers themselves.

I have come to believe that simply telling another person that they must forgive those who have wronged them, especially if they have been deeply abused and mistreated, can be incredibly destructive, especially if it is done without compassion and understanding of that person's position. Many of these people are already struggling with deep feelings of self-loathing, inadequacy, and impotence due to feeling completely powerless to be able to stop those who have deeply wronged them. Simply dumping, "You need to forgive your abusers!" onto these people is only going to frustrate them even more and can actually make them feel as if they are being re-abused. They often already feel they have been deeply mistreated and left to deal with the damage, while their abusers walk away seemingly scot–free. Just being told, "You must forgive them," is only going to reinforce this and add to their already powerful sense of injustice. You cannot just tell these people to let go of their hate, as they can often feel as if their hate is all that they have left to hold on to, to stop them from feeling like a total failure because of what has happened to them.

People who have been abused need to feel they are safe to express their true feelings about those who have wronged them without the threat of others turning against them. They need to get their frustrations out in the open and work through them and heal them. They do need to confess forgiveness—as it is a decision—but that needs to go hand-in-hand with having others around them who are willing to hear them out as they work through what has happened to them. And then they need to know how to get through the pain that they are in.

I learned that although God was calling me to forgive, God brings about consequences for people's actions, and that those who have wronged me will eventually be forced to answer to God for what they have done. I realized that until this happens for them, they are living in limbo, and that they are wasting their energy trying to manage whatever it is that they carry within their own heart. Being in a position where you are forced to walk through it and confront it, is actually far better. I learned that all would be revealed in time, as was shown to me in the following scripture:

> For there is nothing hidden that will not be disclosed, and nothing concealed that will not be known or brought out into the open.
>
> —LUKE 8:17

The truth cannot be hidden forever, and it was best for me to start learning the truth now rather than wasting years in limbo trying to manage the truth about myself that I refused to face.

Once I became aware of these things I began to find the process of forgiveness much easier. Though I still struggle to some degree in this department, I have come a long way, and I have learned a lot by having to walk through the process of having to forgive others. By no means was it easy, but it was a powerful learning experience for me. I can honestly say that without God putting me in the dark places where I was surrounded by offences and having nowhere else to go but within, I would not have come to a place of enlightenment and peace, as I am beginning to experience in my life now.

LEARNING TO GIVE UP THE NEED
TO CONTROL EVERYTHING

I have heard and read many things about managing OCD, but ultimately none of those theories satisfied me as I yearned for a life free from the powerful fears that controlled my existence, not trying to simply manage these feelings. I wanted them to be gone, not just kept in check. I found that with everything that God showed me in regard to the deep and complicated issues within my life, my fears would gradually begin to cease and obsessive behavior was no longer needed as often or to the same degree. Of course, this was a process, and the deeper I went, the more painful it got and the stronger the desire to partake in obsessive behavior became. However, eventually through guidance from the Spirit of God and my own insight, I was able to break through these issues quicker and move on.

I began to learn to see fears for what they were, and instead of running off to do what they said in obedience I began to learn that the problem was really the fear itself. This knowledge, as well as the tools to think with, which God granted me over the years, helped me to break the powerful constriction of fear over my life. I learned that letting go of control was not something that happened overnight or something that came solely out of a decision that I made. I learned that it was a gradual process of learning to give up control piece by piece. It needed to be this way, or I would have quickly become overwhelmed. God helped me to turn every last bit of fear that fueled my controlling behavior into peace and knowledge through helping me to face my fears head on and explore them instead of running from them.

Whenever I felt that someone around me was acting in a bullying or controlling manner, it was like a bomb went off inside me, and I would become almost uncontrollably angry, although I did not always openly express it. I eventually began to realize that my own desires to control people and environments and keep the truth about me suppressed were manifesting in my own heart. Instead of fueling me to partake in controlling activities, they were manifesting because I saw someone else doing it. The full extent of my anger and hatred toward people and circumstances that I perceived to be selfish and controlling was actually generated by my own controlling desires working in reverse. It was far easier to blame someone else for my own feelings and perceptions rather than take a look inside myself and ask why I was feeling so strongly about matters.

I was forced to face up to the feelings that fueled my desire to control things through aggression and intimidation. I began to realize that I actually felt very powerless, helpless, and extremely weak. These feelings caused me to feel deeply inadequate and completely unable to take charge of anything in my life and change things if I felt that I needed to. I felt as if I had no choice but to go with things as they were and that nothing I could ever do would change anything. When I was faced with a situation where I felt that I could control someone or something and get away with it, these feelings would translate through highly aggressive, restrictive, and controlling actions. It was like I was subconsciously saying, "I can't control my life or anything in it, and I cannot stop bad things from happening to me, as I am too little and too weak and too powerless. I feel inadequate beyond belief for these things. However, I sense that I can control this person or situation, and because of that I will absolutely and completely smother them in every way possible, because perhaps the more that I do that, the less inadequate I feel, and I will finally feel as if I can control something after all."

I tried to build up my own world where everything inside it went exactly according to the plan that I had set for it, and there was never any deviation whatsoever. I struggled to control my frustration when this bubble was pierced, and I was forced to face up to the reality that there were many things in my life that I had no control over whatsoever. As long as I continued to live in my little bubble where I controlled absolutely every aspect of everything I was never going to achieve peace, as all I was doing was living in denial. I tried to pull people into this bubble as well, and a huge part of my rage was the realization that people would not do exactly as I had told them to do. It was like I was saying to them, "I've pulled you into this bubble. Now I expect you to do as you are told," and I just expected that my will would be obeyed. The more that people refused to obey what I expected of them (which was completely understandable) the more I felt as if they stood against me in defiance.

Subsequently, I would get more and more frustrated

and angry, so therefore the more I would subsequently try to control them. Whenever I felt that something was important to me I would go out of my way to completely control every aspect of the environment which related to what I felt was important to me, and I would react badly if I ever felt that my control was threatened or ignored. I realized that a lot of the anger came from the fact that I perceived others to be far freer from the need to control than I was, and I resented their ability to be able to disobey me when I laid ridiculous demands upon them. On the other hand, I felt that if any demands were ever laid on me, I felt obliged to obey them due to these same feelings working in reverse, regardless of how ridiculous the demands were.

I knew deep down that I could never stifle another person's free will completely, nor could I ever control what was happening in someone else's mind. Nonetheless, once I obtained a sense of control, there was a powerful fear that would surface of losing the control that I already had, so I would have to continually build on that sense of control through further actions—often actions of anger and aggression. The more I felt afraid that others would rebel against me and try to come out from under my control, the more aggression I would use in order to keep them there. The more aggression I used, the farther I got from the message that was holding the pain captive in my heart, and the farther I got from the message, the worse I felt. The worse I felt, the more aggression I used. It was a horrible, vicious, and destructive cycle.

In nearly every fear I experienced, there was an

element of truth in it that prevented me from just discounting the fear altogether. For example, I greatly feared that someone would break into my house and steal my belongings. This mentality was reinforced as I thought back to times in my life where things were stolen from me because I had been careless. However, instead of listening to the fear and doing what it told me to do, I realized I had to see the fear for what it was and face the message that was in the pain instead of just obeying.

I realized that my fears of not being able to change anything actually came out of a powerful sense of rebellion in my own life, which had been so repressed I had almost blocked it out of my conscious mind. I began to discover that I had always hated laws and rules, even if I never openly expressed it. I always enjoyed having something to fight against. I realized that my feelings of complete inadequacy when it came to trying to control situations came through the rebellion in my life working in reverse. As strongly as I internally embraced rebellious behavior, I also feared it being used against me. Realizing this helped me to feel more comfortable with being assertive in situations, rather than doing my best to be as overpowering and controlling as possible like I used to. It also helped me to realize that I could be assertive without awakening rebellion against me. Trying to control situations as much as possible was my way of stifling the rebellion in my own life—one that would never succeed.

Throughout all this I realized just how deeply the need for control ran in my life and just how subtle it was. I realized how much energy had gone into trying to support this fruitless way of life and how much time I had wasted over the years. I remembered my younger days, the anger and intimidation I tried to use against people while playing sports as a child, the controlling manner I used to treat my friends with as a child, and the passive and timid behavior I continually used against people I believed were more powerful than I was in order to get them to like me. Looking back now, I realized just how hopeless all of this was and how my own blindness to the truth was slowly destroying my life. I know that unless I had committed myself to Christ and began to allow Him to change my heart I probably never would have even realized what I was really doing and would have wasted my whole life through trying to control things I couldn't control at all. Ultimately I would have died worn out and unsatisfied. This realization spurred me toward journeying through these hard places with God—painful as it was—because I knew that it was the only path where I would find what I was really looking for at the other end: peace.

I learned that there are some things in life that need to be controlled and that control is not always a bad thing, depending on the circumstances. For example, if someone was trying to hurt me or my family, I had every right to take control of the situation to stop them. There is, however, a huge difference between legitimate and illegitimate control. Legitimate control is necessary and something every person needs to be capable of. Illegitimate control is about stifling everything around you and within yourself in order to keep your own darkness restrained. I was deeply entrenched in behavior based in illegitimate control, which is what I needed to give up. I needed to learn a healthy balance between situations that required a sense of control and situations that I just needed to let go of.

As time went on and I learned to heal with the help of God, I discovered a wonderful thing: letting go of the need to control everything was happening automatically, and I was slowly becoming more balanced in my thinking. I would often see a situation where I would previously have responded with fear and anxiety exploding within me and driving me to go and do something to fix it, whereas instead of that I now felt a sense of peace and release. I would also feel less guilty and fearful when taking a stance of legitimate control.

Breaking the Power of Addiction

There was never going to be a quick fix to this stronghold in my life. Addiction for me was not made up of any one particular issue but rather many issues which would all translate through whatever different outlet I felt could fulfill my needs at the time.

I tried many different techniques to help me break the power of addiction in my life, especially when it came to cigarette smoking as a teenager. Before I became a Christian I had wanted to kick this habit, and even though I could go for long periods without giving in to the desire to start smoking again it would only end up being a matter of time before I would fall back into the same old trap as before.

Shortly after my eighteenth birthday I received an invite to go to church with my mother, and I decided to ask for prayer against smoking in my life to see if it would help me kick the habit for good. After receiving prayer I found immediately that the desire to smoke that had plagued me for so long was finally gone. Through the defeat of this one addiction that had held me prisoner for so long I began to finally believe that there was actually a way out for me after all and that I could truly be free at last. The following scripture really spoke to me in regard to this: "Not by might nor by power, but by my Spirit, says the LORD" (Zech. 4:6). God was telling me that I would find freedom from addictive behavior through Him and the tools that He gave me to think with.

Though the desire to smoke cigarettes was gone, the other addictive behavior I held for so long was still very present in my life. It was often very subtle and would latch on to things without me even realizing it. I would often find myself completely obsessed with different bands or computer games, and although I didn't realize it at the time I now know that these obsessions were a part of the addictive behavior I held within myself. Using the tools that God had given me to think with, I began to focus on the emotional driving forces behind the addictive behavior rather than just to remove the outlet for it. Doing that would only give the appearance of the addiction being dealt with and would not actually solve anything internally.

I like to use the analogy of a motorboat when I am speaking about this subject. Imagine that there is a motorboat that is automatically set to steer to the right. I might be able to grab the steering wheel and use all of my strength to force it to turn left, but because the steering is automatically set to turn right it will take every last ounce of my strength to keep it going left. Eventually I am going to begin to get tired, and the motorboat is going to start going to the right until it will finally end up turning right again—and I am sitting in the boat feeling utterly defeated. I was fighting a losing battle the entire time, and all of that energy was for nothing. The function that forces the boat to turn right automatically needs to be shut off before it can be steered in a different direction.

I have realized that addictive behavior functions in much the same manner. Trying to cut off the addiction by just trying to shut off the outworking of it is going to fail. The root cause of the addiction needs to be addressed for healing to be able to happen, and then the outworking will no longer be present, as it is no longer needed. My addictions toward different issues in my life were never going to be solved through simply cutting off the outlets they utilized. I needed to learn to face the source of what was driving this obsessive behavior and deal with the feelings that gave it power. It was never going to be an easy journey as I found that I could conjure up all kinds of excuses to justify my own behavior, but deep down in my heart of hearts I knew that I had a problem that needed to be resolved.

The more I began to use the techniques that God had given me to think with, the less I began to feel that I needed these vices in my life. Addiction was beginning to dissipate automatically as I embraced the process of change from the inside out. I would find that relapses could happen at times. However, I realized that I was not going backward when this happened; I was actually going deeper. And now that I had moved on through one layer of fuel for the addictions that had driven me for so long, I was now being confronted with another one. Learning to see these situations for what they were—going deeper with God, rather than feeling defeated or that I was going backwards—helped me enormously to see any new infatuation or addiction for what it truly was. They also helped me hugely to not give up and continue onward with my journey of freeing myself from these powerful, consuming desires.

OVERCOMING RELATIONSHIP ADDICTION

Relationship addiction proved to be a very difficult emotional stronghold to overcome. It had plagued my life for as long as I could remember and often felt like a mountain that could never be climbed.

Once I properly began my Christian walk I initially found it very difficult to try to face this issue, and often God would try to bring it up in my life through potential rejection, confrontation, or violence that I felt I could not control. Instead of remaining in a place where I was able to feel and therefore face the feelings, I would immediately retreat into a passive attitude to try and control the situation to stop any potential harm from coming upon me. I found myself in this place time and time again throughout my Christian walk—sometimes for prolonged periods of time.

A few years ago I found myself working for a local telecommunications company. The business mainly sold cellular phones, but the business also handled a lot of repairs and other problems for the biggest telecommunications provider in New Zealand. This was by far my most challenging environment in regard to the relationship addiction issues. I found myself dealing with hostility and frustration aimed in my direction almost on a daily basis. Most of my behavior in this environment involved me trying to maintain composure by being overly nice. Some people took advantage of this and sensed that they could treat me badly without any fear of repercussion—something I had also been guilty of doing. Being a very small workplace, there was no real place that I could run and hide, yet I could not bring myself to face what was happening within me, as I felt overwhelmed most of the time. I often felt unable to grasp what I was feeling. I could not resign from the job, as I would have had no income in order to pay the rent, and God did not open any other doors at the time, because He wanted me there. It was extremely difficult, but there was no other way.

Through God's grace and the support of friends and family I managed to get through this immensely difficult time in my life. However, I found myself consumed with anger and frustration about what I had experienced in this environment. Most of the anger was directed toward myself for feeling so unable to take any kind of an authoritative stance while I was there and for letting myself be mistreated so badly.

However, God was faithful to me, and He began to show me what was happening in my heart. Whenever I found myself in this mind-set, God would remind me that this situation had been used as a trigger for other issues and that finding the answer would come through exploring the feelings rather than trying to avoid them or playing the blame game. This was difficult to grasp, as it is with any painful situation. It is far easier to attack the situation that has brought up the feelings rather than face the feelings themselves. However, it was the only way through.

God showed me that my wanting to be nice in order to keep people around was based in fear of abandonment and idolatry. The fear revolved around a sense that I had to control people and the circumstances around me in order to keep people from turning against me and leaving me. Because I knew that I could not control their free will, my mission was to control everything else around them to influence their judgment of me. The message deeply imprinted in the fear was this: "I can't lose you no matter what. I need you. I can't survive without you. However, I know that you do not need me or care about me. If I stand up to you, then I am throwing this issue into the wind, and I am letting go of control if I express my anger toward you honestly. I will be throwing this relationship away if I get angry, and that is not something I can lose. If you leave me or turn against me, then I will die. There is no life without you, and I am desperately afraid of death, which I know will come upon me if you leave. So I will control things in order to stop you from leaving me."

I feared that someone would manipulate and push their way into my life and continue to knock at the door of my heart until I finally dropped my guard and opened it to them and gave them access to some of the most sensitive areas of my heart. I feared that once they had gotten hold of some of these deep and intimate details, they would turn and run out of my life with them. The farther they ran, the more it would hurt, as I would not only feel the pain of something precious to me having left me but it would get worse the more they moved away from me. I feared that I would then become a complete wreck by trying to chase after them to bring back these parts of my life. This would make things worse for myself in the process and further open me up to people I did not believe could be trusted. I feared that this desperate state of trying to regain what was lost would lead to me being pushed further toward destruction instead of helping me come back from it. These issues were not necessarily a reflection of reality. However, they felt very real to me.

These issues would trigger when confrontation came

and would manifest in the form of anxiety, which would cause me to act passively in order to try to sedate what I was feeling. The anxiety was caused by the issue arising and me not confronting the message. I would project this negative belief system onto nearly anyone I met—and the working environment at the telecommunications company brought it right to the surface. The abandonment was something that had always been a part of my life. Once I realized that this was the issue I had been facing, I saw the patterns throughout my whole life. Facing the message in this fear was healing in itself. However, I needed to continue to work through the emotions that I carried within myself due to the outworking of this fearful behavior over the years.

The idolatry part came from a number of different sources. It was another thing that I had carried within myself from birth. However, it was reinforced by bullying that I experienced at schools, as well as the victim mentality I carried within myself. God revealed to me that I saw other people as far more valuable, important, and powerful than I was. In fact, I worshiped others as gods. The worse they treated me, the more I saw them as powerful and confident people, so the more I worshiped them. The aggression and disrespect I used against people came about when I felt that others were in awe of me and worshiping me. Once again, it was this same stronghold working in reverse.

The idea that I could do something to a "god" that could anger them or cause them to turn against me was absolutely unthinkable. It felt as though they ruled over my life with an iron fist of anger and violence. I felt that there was no way that I could ever overthrow them, for I would be destroyed if I tried. That created a strong sense of hopelessness and despair. I felt that if I were to become angry at one of these so-called gods I would basically be signing my own death sentence, so I would keep quiet and do what I was told in order to protect myself from the discomfort of having to face these emotions.

Once I realized what was happening I confessed it to God and asked for His forgiveness for this sin of idolatry. Once that happened it was like the people I had put on such high pedestals went from being terrifying, awe-inspiring, God-like figures that could destroy me in seconds to mere mortals, ordinary human beings like myself. They were more than capable of giving me the respect I deserved as a human being and were certainly not to be worshiped; respected, yes—but not worshiped.

Realizing the extent of these issues helped me to begin to establish proper emotional boundaries and helped greatly to dissipate my fear of anger and confrontation. I went from hating the time I spent at the telecommunications job to thanking God for the tremendous insight and experience that this opportunity gave me. It was not easy—but it was the right thing.

LEARNING TO OVERCOME
OPPRESSION AND SELF-DIVISION

I believe self-division was a big driving factor regarding the OCD tendencies in my life. I have mentioned previously regarding how deeply oppressed I felt and how I felt as if I was living in an emotional and spiritual prison. This was one of the very first things God allowed to surface in my life when I rededicated my life to Him. However, I did not understand it to begin with, and I used to blame God for the way I was feeling when He was trying to bring this up. It was not until recently that I was really able to start getting an idea of what was really happening with this huge issue in my life.

I always used to think that these were external forces at work against me. However, this was not the truth. It felt very much like there was a whole other person inside of me who deliberately and knowingly stood against me and everything that I did, and that this person wanted me to hate them because it made them happy to know that I was suffering because of them. God showed me that due to this being in my heart I was divided against myself, and this was why I was not prospering emotionally and spiritually. This so-called alter-ego would stand against me in every possible way that it could and would often set me up for sabotage in my personal life. I would often say and do things that would bring shame upon me, and I did not fully understand why, yet I could not help doing it. I believe God has shown me that this all came down to me being divided against myself. Jesus addressed this issue very clearly: "If a kingdom is divided against itself, that kingdom cannot stand" (Mark 3:24). I was divided against myself internally.

I was forced to realize that the desires to control, manipulate, and oppress that caused the powerful self-rejection and division that I hated were actually desires that I was embracing deep within my own heart and mind. I was once again being forced to realize that I was a tyrant. As I looked back upon my life I realized just how true this was and just how strongly rooted in my life these desires were. If these desires to control, manipulate, stifle, oppress, and intimidate did not have something or someone that they could target externally to attack through me, then they would simply turn on the one who was carrying them around in the first place—me. It was like I had desperately tried to distance myself from these desires to control, which I hated so much, but seeing as they were a part of me I was turning against myself as well. Trying to run from them—and therefore myself—was never going to work. I needed to learn to stand and face the ugly truth about my own heart in this regard.

God did not show me this internal ugliness about myself in judgment or condemnation. Rather, He provided me with a way through it using the tools I had been given to think with. I had to realize that I wanted to be God myself and that I wanted to be in control of everything. I wanted to force the entire world to answer to me. I didn't care who hated me for doing it or who would be upset, just so long as I was in the untouchable position of control and domination. I enjoyed being in charge and knowing that other people were angry at me but powerless to do anything about it. It was a horrible type of greed that was just out to stifle, manipulate, and dominate everything in its path.

It was like I was sitting on a high horse laughing at people around me who were scrabbling around in the darkness and full of anger and frustration because it was me who put them there, and they could not do anything about it. The more they hated me, the more I just laughed at them. I felt as if the world had rejected me, so I had rejected the world in turn, but I craved power so that I could force them to fear me and therefore submit to me and do as I told them. I hated this monstrous thing that tried to control me so desperately, and tried so hard to cut off my every escape route—but the truth hit me like a ton of bricks. I hated tyranny and oppression more than anything in the world, only because I carried this sense of tyranny within myself. This monster I hated so much was none other than me, a part of me that I tried to ignore and pretend wasn't really there. In doing so, I gave it more room to move.

God gave me three names of the spiritual forces that I carried within myself. The first name was the spirit of Antichrist. It was Satan's counterfeit version of Christ Himself. However, unlike Christ, it was abusive, legalistic, controlling, and violent and would abuse its power to no end. This spirit would lie and convince me that it was God and that it had all of God's power, so I should fear it beyond measure, as it hated me and wanted to destroy me. It would lie to me and tell me, "You think things are hard for you at the moment? This is only the tip of the iceberg. You can't fight me because I rule your whole life. I have unlimited firepower at my disposal, guaranteed to cut you down. I am your god, and there is no way that you can ever overthrow me. You have no choice but to submit—or die." There was no mercy, no love, and no forgiveness in this spirit, and it kept me in prison emotionally for years. I do not believe I was possessed by this spirit, as my spirit was made whole by Christ when I accepted Jesus as my Savior. However, it was definitely controlling a dark part of my soul that had not yet been submitted unto God.

The second name was the spirit of Goliath. Goliath was a biblical character that tormented the Israelites (God's chosen people) with continual threats of violence and war. His huge size (reportedly over nine feet tall) aided in his ability to intimidate others. The spirit of Goliath had ruled over my life for as long as I could remember. Whenever I tried to fight back against anyone or change anything I would feel the overwhelming pressure of the spirit of Goliath telling me to back down. Because it was hidden in darkness and I was not aware of its name, it was able to intimidate me. It felt like I was standing against a monster that was far bigger than me and could crush me in an instant. Part of the outworking of this spirit's negative influence was my dread, which was associated with doing anything wrong. I felt very strongly that any sort of failure gave the spirit of Goliath room to condemn and crush me with an unlimited supply of cruelty and condemnation. Therefore, I tried desperately to be perfect, and if I perceived that someone else was weaker than I was I would often demand complete perfection from them as well, with serious consequences to follow if my rules were not obeyed. Once again, if it wasn't working against me to destroy me, it was working through me to destroy others.

The third name was Demonic Guardian Angel. Guardian angels are godly beings sent to protect and watch over people. They encourage people when to move forward with different things and when to hold back. This spirit was the satanic counterfeit of God's guardian angels. It would pressure me into moving forward when God wanted me to hold back and pressure me into holding back when God wanted me to move forward. It was out to destroy me from within and wanted to sabotage everything I had in my life in order to stop me from fulfilling God's purpose. I remember I would be standing and talking to people that I knew and cared about, and all of a sudden I would get this overwhelming urge to punch them in the face or spit at them or swear at them. This desire did not come from me at all, and it was deeply upsetting, as I knew that the moment I let go of the reins I held on to so tightly this spirit would take control and do its best to ruin everything I held dear. This spirit had dedicated its entire life to controlling me and stifling me and would use every opportunity it could to reassert control and dominance over my heart.

The fear of the influence and control of these spirits played a huge part in my struggles with anxiety and my desire to control things and people at all times. They greatly influenced the desire I had to be perfect. I felt that the moment I let go of control they would take over and destroy everything. Unfortunately, trying to become perfect was never going to destroy the influence of these dark spirits in my life, as I was trying to externally control and satisfy something that I carried within myself. I was continually fighting a losing battle. Deep down I knew this; however, I didn't know what else I could do, so I just kept trying to be perfect in order to stifle the way I was already feeling. The powerful fear of the influence of these spirits unfortunately cut me off from being able to receive the grace, love, and forgiveness of God. To be able to receive grace and forgiveness, one's soul must be open and broken before God. I was terrified of feeling open and broken before anyone, as I expected the crushing hammer of oppression to come and destroy me if I entered into this emotional landscape.

I confessed to God for harboring these spirits within myself, and I asked for His forgiveness for allowing them to operate in and through me and torment others as well. I asked for prayer from a trusted Christian mentor, and I also asked God's forgiveness for allowing these spirits to distort my perspective of what God was truly like. However, God did not condemn me. Quite the opposite. I felt that He was pleased with me for learning to face up to this horrible aspect of myself that I dreaded having to look at. I realized that this had not been happening in my life externally, and these desires, although hidden, were very strong and were only ever waiting for an opening. If I had got into a position of some sort of power with this kind of corruption embedded deeply within my heart, it would just be a matter of time until they came forth and started to dictate my actions.

This was a very sobering lesson for me to learn. I am glad I learned about this ugliness within myself before it was able to take hold and do some real damage through me. I am grateful that God was gracious enough to teach me this before I began to reap some very bad fruit as a result. Though digging into this issue was very painful and a very isolating process, the peace that began to come over me once I faced up to this and asked for God's forgiveness was amazing, and I felt the ugliness and hostility begin to dissipate. The peace that was coming was the "peace of God, which surpasses all understanding" (Phil. 4:7, ESV). I had been attempting to create peace by stifling these desires, or even worse, trying to fulfill them throughout my entire life. I am so thankful I was able to learn that peace comes from the release of self rather than the exaltation of self.

COMING TO THE END OF MYSELF

Several years ago I received a prophetic word from a good friend of mine. He spoke over my life and said to me, "God is going to allow you to be completely broken. However, out of that place of brokenness there is an amazing healing and testimony that is going to come forth." Though I didn't like the sound of the prophecy,

I put it into the back of my mind and didn't reject the word that was given to me.

In July 2011 I spent a few days wearing a pair of shoes that had holes in the bottom. I only noticed this when I got home from work and realized that my socks were wet, as it had been raining. Because I had been wearing wet socks inside my shoes the socks rubbed against my feet and caused these painful sores where the skin had rubbed off. I tried to ignore the pain and let it heal on its own, but it wouldn't. I tried rubbing ointment on the wounds, but that just seemed to make it worse.

Eventually the pain became so bad that I found myself limping everywhere, so I finally decided to get myself to the doctor and get my feet looked at. He said that they were quite badly infected and prescribed me a strong antibiotic to knock the infection out. Though the antibiotic knocked out the infection, it also had terrible side effects, as I believe I was allergic to it. It took away my appetite completely, so I wasn't able to eat for several days afterward. It also gave me a bad bout of insomnia, so I wasn't able to sleep for days either. It also shrunk my stomach. I couldn't even drink a glass of orange juice without wanting to throw it back up.

One morning after three days of being on this antibiotic I went to the toilet, and I found evidence that my old stomach ulcer I suffered many years back had begun bleeding again. This sent me into a frenzy of fear, and I drove straight to the hospital, where I was informed that I was once again bleeding internally. Realizing that this old condition had flared up again brought back a lot of painful memories of the first time the ulcer bled, where I had to be rushed to hospital for an emergency gastroscopy, which took several months to fully recover from. My mind began spiraling out of control into a place of fear and dread of having to face all of this again.

Though the ulcer only bled slightly and healed itself, I began noticing major changes after all of this had happened. I noticed that my moods were considerably darker than before and that I would often find myself crying uncontrollably for no reason. My appetite didn't return properly, which was highly unusual for me, as I am a very big eater by nature. I began to feel more and more disinterested in usual activities that I enjoyed and found that my energy levels were considerably lower than usual. I also picked up a bad flu throughout this time and found myself awake, often throughout the night, coughing furiously, sometimes for hours on end. Antibiotics for the cough didn't seem to help, and it got to the point where I couldn't keep food down because I would just cough until I was sick. This, compiled with the physical exhaustion of not being able to eat properly and recovering from the side effects of the antibiotics, led to me losing quite a bit of weight.

I was also getting through a very busy period at my job, and I was struggling with a large issue of tension in my heart that I just couldn't resolve. No matter how hard I tried and how much insight I threw at it, it just wouldn't budge. I begged God for answers to this tension, but He was silent. This added to the decrease in my enjoyment of life and felt very discouraging, as I had taken great pride in my own ability to control and identify what was happening in my own heart, and now it just wasn't working at all. All of these issues compiling upon me at once led to a decrease in my output at my job, which made me feel worse yet again, as I now felt I was failing my employers.

One night, after a social situation went contrary to my expectations, I had about three or four hours of sleep, all of which were filled with horrible nightmares. The rest of the time I was awake, coughing violently. When I awoke the following morning, I was completely at the end of my rope for the first time ever. I was at the point where I was deliberately planning to take my own life, as I was just overwhelmed and exhausted and no longer felt able to cope. I realized I had just experienced a complete nervous breakdown.

My mother made an emergency trip to my house immediately and sat down with me and prayed that evening. As we sought God together she asked me what I was feeling, and I found myself saying that I felt like I had to be in control of things at all times, because if I lost control of anything I would surely die. The Holy Spirit revealed to us both that I was struggling with a spiritual inheritance of death, which had come down the generational lines from an abortion attempt against an unborn baby decades before I was even conceived. The baby survived but was deeply traumatized by the terror of facing such rejection and death in a place that was supposed to be safe. It was also deeply aware of its own helplessness to do anything about the attempt on its life.

This incident had never happened to me personally—but the effect of this spiritual inheritance on my body and mind was enormous.

I realized that I had built my whole life around this powerful fear of death, and the terror of being unable to stop it had led me to want to control the entire universe in order to keep myself safe. The only safety that I knew was in control, which of course was a lie, but it was so strongly rooted I just believed it and acted out of it without truly knowing what it was. The control would manifest in any means necessary to keep me safe— whether that involved controlling circumstances, others, or myself. I also realized that this inheritance caused me to have no value of human life and to see human beings as worthless and dispensable, as the baby believed that it must be worth nothing if its own mother tried to murder it. This abortion issue was the root of the deep tension I was struggling with. Though the fear of death was not based in reality, because it was strongly rooted in a darkened part of my heart it still had influence. It was a lie that I had believed my whole life, and that lie had kept me wound very tightly and acted as a primary catalyst in my mental health issues.

I was forced to resign from my job as a result and go on a sickness benefit in order to take the time to fully rest and recover. Though the spiritual part of the issue had been dealt with, the recovery process was only just beginning. I had to work through the lies that were compacted deeply within the recesses of my soul that this inheritance of death had been rooted in. There were other spiritual issues God showed me that had also come down through the generational lines that contributed to my powerful need to control things and feelings of absolute terror at facing situations that I couldn't control.

Facing these lies that I had built my entire life upon was a painful and frustrating process. There were times when I would want to lash out in anger at what had happened to me in my circumstances, and there were times when I just wanted to give up on trying to get better. It was like facing the psychological equivalent of a root canal on a daily basis. However, God was faithful. I realized that He allowed all of these things to happen so that I would be put in a place with no distractions so that I could fully face and work through these issues. As I began to unpack these deeply rooted lies and fears, I began to sense a strength emerging within me that I had never experienced before.

It was almost like I needed to come to a place of absolute, utter defeat before I could start to live in victory. God had been allowing me to slide down the dark and slippery slope because He wanted me to come to the end of myself so that I could face these feelings and therefore be free of them. I had been spending all of my energy trying to clamber back up the slope when, as a matter of fact, sliding down to the absolute bottom of it was what God wanted for me, as it was where I needed to be. I believe that once you get to the end of yourself and hit absolute rock bottom, you are in a tremendous place to receive blessing and peace, as from then on, the only way to go is up.

Part Three

OBSERVATIONS AND THEORIES

TRUE CHANGE STARTS FROM WITHIN

As I PROGRESSED farther and farther into my journey and gathered more understanding about myself and what had made me the way I was, I began to look on the outside world with different eyes. From the day that we are born we are exposed, mostly unwillingly, to lies, deceit, and wrong belief structures about ourselves and the world and people around us. Being young and impressionable, we embrace these things and hold them in our hearts very deeply. We build our entire lives on these things, which lurk deep within our subconscious minds, and we keep them down there, as they become too painful to face. So, we set up distractions in our lives in order to protect ourselves from the true nature of what really dwells within us.

This way of thinking creates a culture of so-called needs which very often are not needs at all but simply distractions people want to partake in so that they can turn their eyes away from their own spiritual and emotional reality. Entire businesses and operations in the modern-day world are designed to fulfill these so-called needs, which are ever so present in modern day society. However, fulfilling these "needs" will not really end up helping anyone in the long run. Our whole society has been constructed in this manner—to manage people's pain, darkness, confusion and sin and keep it stuffed away rather than encouraging them to face their demons and embrace the process of change that will bring freedom.

So many people try to change their lives through changing things in their lives—their spouse, job, car, anything. Of course, there are times when these changes are necessary, but I cannot help but wonder just how often change in these areas was not really necessary at all and what really needed to change was within a person's heart, rather than in their circumstances. However, people are not taught this lesson. From day one, our society is constantly inundated with material telling people how they can have better lives if they just do this or do that or buy this or buy that. Advertising works brilliantly in this regard, as it continually encourages people to buy, buy, buy with the promise of satisfaction. But even after buying something there is a very good chance that dissatisfaction will settle in that person's heart, and they will become bored with what they have bought and will need to go back for more—something bigger, something newer, something with more features.

I was very familiar with this way of thinking myself.

I just wanted to feel better, and I would do what I felt was necessary to achieve that. When I was experiencing some of the worst periods of OCD throughout my life, my behavior probably would have baffled those who observed me closely, and they would wonder why I would do some of the things that I did. The answer for me was simple. *I was looking for an emotional release, and I was trying to find it the best way that I knew how.* I believe many people are strongly embedded in this wrong way of thinking and acting without even realizing it. This realization helped me to develop my own theory on how addicts of any kind function. They are simply looking for that very same thing, an emotional release.

It makes sense when you think about it. Why would someone choose to take revenge on someone else when they believe that they have been wronged by them? Why do people blame others for their own feelings rather than take ownership of them, and thus create accusations and even more pain in the world than there is already? Why are people continually dissatisfied with what they have and wanting more, when it will only lead to further dissatisfaction down the road? I believe it is simply because they want a release from what they are feeling within themselves. Why would someone continually take hard drugs, even when they know that they are putting their life in danger and could die? Of course, there are chemical addictions to take into account in regard to this, but emotionally I believe the answer is the same: they see it as something that can help and will give them release, which of course it never will. But they believe that so strongly and refuse to change their thinking. Also, because of the initial good feelings brought on by the drugs, they refuse to let go and dig themselves deeper when they are only trying to find a way out.

This culture of thinking and trying to internalize problems through external circumstances is not really solving any of the problems in our world today but rather covering them up and helping people to stifle them for a time. Change for the better starts from *within* and will then eventually be followed by external change—not the other way around. We will never solve our own problems through trying to blame others for what are actually our own responsibilities, nor will we solve our problems through continued disregard of our own emotions and hearts, and through listening to an increasingly shallow and self-serving society. Acting this way will only continue to add to the cycle of pain and injustice, brokenness, addiction, and confusion so prevalent in modern day society.

Emotional Translation in Modern-day Society

I believe the western world is full of negative emotional translation. It is something that has been programmed into all of us throughout our entire lives. It is so easy to try and pass the blame onto others for our own internal problems, and in many situations people can feel quite justified in blaming someone else for something that is actually within them. They do this because they are only focusing on the external factors at work and refuse to realize that there are also internal factors at work as well.

I experienced this often while working for the telecommunications company. We would often see people come into the shop and yell and carry on at us about problems they were experiencing and needed help with. Even when we would speak to them politely, we would often still be on the receiving end of abuse. I felt that I was being treated unjustly, and I asked myself why people would tend to react so strongly over things that very often were not the fault of anyone who actually worked in the shop. No confrontation was being initiated on our part, so I asked myself how and why people would act with such anger toward me and other shop assistants when we had done nothing to initiate it. I analyzed this and came up with a theory as to why I think this would happen.

It starts off with a problem inside someone's heart and soul that is weighing them down and is quite often unknown to them. Something then happens to them externally that triggers an internal manifestation of this inward problem; in this case, a cell phone stops working when it is needed. The person in question is now emotionally aware of the problem, but in many cases they do not define it and are unable to pinpoint what it is based around. The logical step then for them is to release that internal turmoil that the situation has caused by shouting and screaming at the subject that has manifested the internal turmoil, in this case the cell phone or a representative of the company who supply the cell phones. That, for me, was the reason we would often see people coming into the shop and shouting and screaming because their phone was not working. In most cases it was nothing to do with us, and even when it was, the emotional response from the customer was often unnecessary.

What I believe the customer was saying to us subconsciously through their ranting and raving was that they could not deal with their emotions being surfaced and could not deal with having to truly face themselves. Rather than take the more difficult but necessary road of defining the problem and trying to take a second to think clearly about things and truly ask themselves if there was more going on than the simple fact of a phone not working correctly, they take the easy road by finding someone to blame who they can feel justified in blaming and demand that their problem be fixed.

The problem with this theory is that even though the circumstance may be fixed, the problem itself, which is actually found within the heart and mind of the person in question, does not change and is buried back down into the subconscious realm. Though they do not realize it, when things like this happen the person in question has been granted a wonderful opportunity to change their own heart for the better and to learn something about themselves in the process that could really enlighten them. However, because it is painful and because they often lack the awareness about themselves to do this, they simply take the easy way out and blame what they think is the cause of the problem, which often creates unnecessary grief for anyone on the other end.

This wrong and shallow way of thinking causes a huge amount of stress in our society. I was no exception myself; I was deeply embedded in this way of thinking when I was growing up and more often than not many people in my life were unfairly wounded by me translating my emotions incorrectly and lashing out at people and circumstances that did not deserve it. It was only once I became a Christian that my mind-set began to change, and I began to learn of the truth of the unseen realm and how to treat people properly. God is in the business of changing hearts and minds in order to bring greater peace into the world. True peace comes from inside oneself, not through external circumstances.

Those who have truly given their lives to Christ must learn to embrace this thinking, which is so backward compared to the thinking drilled into people's minds by modern society. Modern society in many ways tells people to look for peace and happiness in external circumstances; hence the abundance of consumerism. Christ's way of thinking, which He passes on to those who follow Him, encourages the individual to seek out true, lasting peace and understanding through looking honestly into the mirror and journeying with God through the parts of themselves they would rather avoid. This is where true character is developed, and character is something becoming more and more absent in modern society.

Embracing a New Pattern of Thinking

God's way of thinking is a total contradiction to the world's way of thinking. The world's way of thinking encourages dishonesty, shallowness, irresponsibility, and pride. God's way of thinking encourages honesty, depth, personal responsibility, and humility. Learning to function with this new type of thinking can be very difficult and a very lonely experience. I believe that this is where a lot of new Christians fall away from the faith, both young and old. When Christ comes into the life of an individual, He seeks to change the person into something new—from within their own heart.

My experiences as a new Christian were very difficult. The Holy Spirit was seeking to change me from within and was using external circumstances to surface the internal trauma and pain I had stored up inside me. He wanted me to work through it and learn how to be healed, which we find in the following scripture:

> Do not conform any longer to the pattern of this world, but be transformed by the renewing of your mind.
>
> —Romans 12:2

However this immediately clashed with my old mind-set saying that everything is external and if hard times come, take the easy way out and get away from them as soon as possible. Many times I felt very much that I wanted to run away, as it was easier. New Christians are some of the most vulnerable people around, as more often than not they do not understand the full magnitude of what has taken place within them and what God is now trying to do. They become angry and discouraged and fall away from the faith.

I first looked upon changing my thinking as something to do every once in a while. It took me a long time to realize it was something that needed to happen on a daily basis and would continue for the rest of my life. God speaks of streams of living water that flow from within the believer. I find this phrase interesting, as streams are never stationary. They are always flowing forward. Water becomes stagnant if it does not move and quickly becomes vulnerable to disease. I believe that this verse speaks of the journey of the true believers in Christ who have been changed internally by His Spirit. They are always moving forward, like the stream, going from glory to glory. I learned that God would always be changing me for the better so that I would reflect His glory better and that I would subsequently learn more about myself in the process.

To this day, both sides of the coin are present in my life. There are still parts of myself that I do not know, and I still regularly battle temptation to medicate through external sources rather than journey inward and find the answer with God. What I have journeyed through and learned already is continually making itself more and more present in my life, but there is always more to work through. A stream of water does not stop flowing when it hits an obstacle. However, obstacles can hinder the stream or stop it for a time. Still as long as the stream continues to flow from the source, it will find a way through eventually. In much the same way the streams of living water that flow from the heart of the believer do not stop when they hit obstacles—old mind-sets, old feelings previously buried deep within our hearts. As long as we stay connected to the source of the stream, they will continue to pound against the obstacles in our hearts until they are removed.

It can be easy to feel flat and discouraged, but if you are getting through issues and continually hitting more then it means that you are making progress. The deeper the stream goes, the more of the darkness is uncovered, and a little bit more strength is added to the foundation God wants to build in the lives of the believer.

When I mention darkness, I do not necessarily mean evil. Darkness can be a breeding ground for evil, but the definition of darkness is lack of light. God is light. There is no darkness in Him; therefore God is not fazed by the things that we are fazed by, as He knows Himself completely. There is no breeding ground for evil in the heart of God. I believe that God wishes to pass this on to us and wishes to bring us into a real place of enlightenment where we can bring genuine, dependable peace and knowledge to the world through first getting to know ourselves.

My honest belief in regard to Satan, the enemy of God, is that the only power that he has over Christians is the power that we give him. He cannot create darkness; all he can do is use the darkness that is already there. I like to paint a picture of a wall with handholds in it, and

Satan is holding on to these. We can throw everything we like at him while he is there, but he will continue to hang on as long as those handholds are there. If we want to truly rid ourselves of his influence, then we need to kick out his handholds. Once they are gone he will fall, as he has nothing left to hold on to in our lives. The wall describes the heart of a person, and the handholds describe areas of our hearts that have not been dealt with yet. Satan, therefore, is able to hang on to those and use them against us. We can try everything we like to get rid of him, but he will not leave as long as he has those handholds. Once we deal with the darkened area in our hearts that he is holding on to, he loses his handholds and therefore falls.

I believe that it is getting harder and harder to embrace this pattern of self-reflective thinking in modern-day society as the world seeks to distance itself from its own reality even further. It can be very easy for Christians to also be swept up in this mentality of distraction and medicating issues. God's challenge of facing the truth was never an easy one to begin with, and as the world progresses farther toward a culture based entirely on distractions, God's challenge will become harder yet again. However, I believe that God is calling His people to be different and to not be afraid to face the most difficult thing to face in their entire lives—themselves.

Your Heart Defines Your Life

Many times throughout my journey things would happen to me that I absolutely did not understand—including after I rededicated my life to Christ. I faced some horrible trials when I first became a Christian, such as long periods of unemployment and other incredibly painful and uncomfortable scenarios. I knew that God was using these times to test me and discipline me. However, I felt very angry and frustrated, as I basically believed that I was a good person and to begin with. I failed to understand how God could let something so difficult happen to me.

My beliefs about God were true—God is a just God—yet my acknowledgment of myself was far from true. The fact of the matter is, God was using this discipline to show me areas of myself that needed to change, and the discipline was justified, as I had enough darkness and instability in my own heart to justify God reaching down and shaking my life to bring everything to the surface. After a while I came up with this little catch phrase that I believe to be very true: what and who we have in our lives always comes down to what we have in our hearts.

Whether or not we choose to acknowledge this is irrelevant. The Bible tells us that our entire lives are based on what we carry inside our hearts: "Above all else, guard your heart, for it is the wellspring of life" (Prov. 4:23). If one's heart is filled with fear, that person will either have nothing in their life, as they are too afraid to get it, or many things that they are extremely protective and defensive of, as they are terrified that they will lose them. That fear, most of the time, will end up causing them to lose everything, thus justifying the fear in the first place. Even if they manage to retain everything, all they are doing through retaining it is wasting their energy to satisfy a fear that can never truly be satisfied. Even if they give the fear what it wants, there will be no rest in that, and the fear will simply want more. The fearful person needs to realize that his problem and his pain have nothing to do with what he is afraid of losing, but the fear itself. The problem is within him, nowhere else, and until he realizes that he is doomed to a life of dis-satisfaction and continual striving to satisfy something that will never have its fill but will only exhaust him in the process.

An angry, bitter, and hostile person who is constantly confronting people and bullying others will be sur-rounded by people who simply tolerate them and are nice to them out of fear, but there is no genuine love or concern for their well-being if we were to dig a little deeper. That person will find themselves surrounded by false friends and true enemies, and relationships will all be on a slippery slope to failure, regardless of how good they may seem. Regardless of how carefully they hide what is inside them, and how strongly they try to justify it with other parts of their life that are good, eventually what they have within them will destroy them from the inside out. The distractions they use to cover up their true selves have use-by dates. They simply cannot last forever, as truth cannot be hidden. It can be smothered for a while, but eventually truth will win out. Until then their entire life is a ticking time bomb. Being in a place of smug comfort and feeling that you can get away with it forever and that you can keep the bitterness stored up inside you without consequences is a very dangerous place to be in, as these people, plainly and simply, will not see the disasters that are poised to overtake them.

If a person does not believe that other people care about them, it really doesn't matter how many people gather around them and say that they care about them. It won't make any difference to the person who believes this, as their own belief that nobody does care is actually cutting them off from being able to receive the care that is given to them. This belief that nobody cares can translate into a person's attitude and the way that they interact with other people. This can cause them to treat others with negativity in the belief that they do not care about them anyway, which can often cause those who do care to respond in a negative manner, which then reinforces the original belief of the person in question. By acting out of their own heart and not dealing with it, people can actually cause their worst fears to come upon them in this manner. This is a very sad fact of life and one I have struggled with very deeply myself, but it is true.

I struggled for a long time with the belief that no one truly cared about me or my feelings and that no one was interested in what I was going through, not even God. Through not dealing with this problem inside my own heart I blocked myself off from receiving the care and support from people around me who genuinely did care—or alienated them altogether. It did not help my own cause one bit.

The heart is the wellspring of life, and what we have in our lives is based on what we have in our heart. Very often something very hard can happen to a person who thinks they are good through and through, and they question why. I believe in this instance we need to dig a little deeper and search our heart, ask ourselves hard questions, and ask God to reveal our true nature and our true heart to us. Very often we will find that there is something inside of us that we did not know was there and in many ways could well have caused this thing to come upon us.

God is just, and God does not let anything happen for no reason. I have learned to think differently now. If I ever face anything in my life that is painful and hard to deal with, instead of getting frustrated that it has happened I have now learned to acknowledge that God is in control and that there is something that I can learn from this. I no longer agree with the phrase "sometimes bad things happen to good people." The way I see it, God can use everything that happens to us to teach us something that we need to know about God, life, others, and ourselves.

Discovering the Purpose of God in All Things

Very often, the purposes of God for our lives in different circumstances can greatly differ from what we expect. It is easy for believers to take a certain situation that they are currently facing at face value, whereas all too often God's purposes for whatever they are facing can be totally different. I faced this a few years back. I had just recently moved to a new city to start a new job, and I was made redundant from the new job that I was about to start due to the business being sold to new owners on the day I was supposed to start with them. I was able to get a decent pay-out from the job I was meant to start at; however, for the next four months I was out of work.

Eventually I was able to get a job at the telecommunications company I mentioned previously doing outbound sales around the area to business clients and individual consumers alike. People told me from day one that they did not feel that this job was suitable for me, and while a small part of me tended to agree with what they were saying, I was in rather desperate need of a job, so I decided to accept the position. The alternative—staying on the unemployment benefit—was not going to be beneficial for me financially.

After the first few days on the job it became glaringly obvious to me that I was somewhat inadequate for the tasks requested of me in this role. I did not have the personality or the temperament to be able to prosper in this environment. However, seeing as I knew that God had opened this door for me and put me there, I decided to stick it out to the best of my abilities. I saw the earning potential that came along with the sales targets that I was set, and I felt sure that, seeing as God was with me, I would be able to hit these targets without any trouble.

However, I was very wrong. The months that followed for me were best described as hell on Earth. The shop environment could become incredibly hostile, and due to my personal struggles I found this very difficult to cope with at the time. The impersonal treatment that I received from the people that came into the store was very difficult for me to cope with. My Christian walk and changing mind-set meant that I was looking at the way people would act and their treatment of others at a far more complex level. To be able to succeed in a job like this I felt very much that I needed to achieve some kind of emotional disconnection to bring myself to a shallow and impersonal level. This was not something I felt I that could achieve, neither did I feel that it was something God wanted me to do.

We were also trying to sell a cellular network that was performing poorly at best, especially in the area that the shop was based, as coverage was not great compared to other areas. Regardless of this, I was still expected to sell it. However, I struggled very much to hit my sales targets. Nothing seemed to go right for me in this place, and I felt as if everything I touched just collapsed. I did not understand this, as I felt very much that God had opened this door for me to be in this job, so I automatically expected to excel at what I was doing. I could not understand why it was not happening and any kind of success just seemed far away for me.

On the way home from a Christian conference one weekend I found myself conversing with God deeply in prayer regarding this subject. I was pouring my heart out to Him as to why I felt so frustrated, why I felt as if things were so hard for me, and how I could not understand why things were going so badly for me in this environment, yet I still had to stay there. God spoke to me—and His words caught me off guard. He simply said, "Maybe you are not supposed to succeed in this role." I knew that this was the voice of God from my own spirit, as not only was it completely removed from what I was initially thinking, but it was like my thought processes came to a grinding halt the moment that I heard these words. My mind cleared in an instant, and I began to think about what I had heard.

I realized that what I had heard was indeed from God and that succeeding in this role was not His plan for me—and that He had another purpose entirely. Though it was good to hear this, as things finally began to make a bit more sense, it was also incredibly difficult for me to hear this, as I was still expected to succeed by my employers. But I had just been told by God that success in this position was not His plan for me. This created a lot of alienation for me, as I knew now that my purpose for being there was different from what they had expected of me. I began to realize that God had put me in this hostile environment for my own spiritual growth and emotional healing. The hostility and negativity of this environment—including the repercussions of not achieving my sales targets—was being used to help me deal with my own heart and become a stronger person.

Of course, my employers did not understand this, and there was no way that I could tell them what was really going on, and that created further discomfort for me. I felt incredibly alone at this point in time, and despite the fact that I was making huge progress in regard to dealing with my emotions and becoming stronger, I was continually faced with more issues within myself that I needed to get through, which was incredibly exhausting. It was painful and distressing to be thrown into an emotionally bleak environment within myself by the hostile, impersonal, and often disrespectful attitudes of many of the people we dealt with.

This continued for months, and the toll on my body and my emotions became heavier and heavier. Workmates I considered friends were often asking me if I was OK, and I found it difficult to shed light on what was really going on for me. Things did not get better for me in this environment. They became progressively worse, despite how much stronger emotionally I had become. Eventually the door finally opened for another job that was far better than the current job I had and far more suitable for me, and I was able to leave the position at the telecommunications company, much to my relief.

As difficult as this environment was for me, I learned a huge amount from it. I learned a lot about myself, and I made some real breakthroughs through some very deeply rooted issues in my life. I struggled with anger and frustration at having been put in this position even long after I had left. However, I slowly began to realize that the work situation had merely triggered issues in my life that needed to be dealt with, and therefore lashing out at the trigger was not going to be beneficial. My initial assumption that God had put me there to succeed was totally wrong, and I realized that God had a far different purpose to what I was initially anticipating. I am reminded of the scripture, "For my thoughts are not your thoughts, neither are your ways my ways, declares the LORD" (Isa. 55:8–9). Through my own prideful expectations, I simply expected to wildly succeed. God wanted to use this situation to humble me and teach me that it was OK to fail.

I also learned that I felt as if I were not worthy of love or acceptance simply because I was me. I felt as if I had to earn my place with everything that I did. When it came to things in life that I knew everything about, this wasn't a problem, as I could easily live up to my own self-expectations. However, when I was faced with something that I could not totally control or learn everything about, I would become sullen and depressed. I felt that there was no way that I could earn my acceptance anymore, so it would just be a matter of time until I was thrown out. Being put in a place where I was pretty much guaranteed to fail forced me to start facing up to this. I could not spend my life working out of a spirit of pride and self-expectation to achieve everything, as that would only ever lead to exhaustion. Learning to fail—as immensely difficult as it was—helped me to begin to learn humility and the simple fact that I could not control absolutely everything around me after all.

I learned from this point on that I should never assume what God is doing in any given situation and that His purposes can be totally different to what we take at face value. Learning this lesson has helped me see my life circumstances through a different set of eyes, and I no longer jump to assumptions as to why I feel God has placed me in different situations.

BUILDING A STRONG FOUNDATION

Jesus spoke on the importance of building a strong foundation. He told the story of a wise man who built his house on the rock and a foolish man who built his house on the sand. As soon as the storms came along, the foolish man's house was destroyed, but the wise man's house stood firm, thanks to its strong foundation. I received a word of prophecy when I was being baptized saying that God was going to build a strong foundation in my life. I didn't really know what this meant at the time, but it was the beginning of a totally new journey in my life.

God wanted me to be strong within my soul and able to withstand the storms of life. I needed to have a strong foundation built into my life to be able to handle these storms when they came upon me. However, my foundation was deeply cracked and broken. Being an anxiety sufferer, as well as all of the other issues I had struggled with throughout the years, I was not a mentally and emotionally strong person. God gave me a vision of cement being poured into the deep cracks in my life in order to fill them in and make them strong and solid once again.

When I was in my late teens to early twenties and still very much a new Christian, many friends of mine were seemingly beginning to live life to the fullest. Friends of mine owned cars and motorcycles, lived out of home, had girlfriends, and were holding down good jobs with fun, freedom, and pleasure on their side. My life was the complete opposite. At nineteen years old I was a university dropout and spent about ten months working two days a week at a supermarket job that I did not enjoy. I lived with my parents, had no girlfriend or driver's license, and found myself continually envying the lifestyles of those around me.

However, as much as I resented it, God had put me in this position for a reason. He was taking away all external distractions to help me to delve deep into my own heart to begin to change my life from the inside out. This was the beginning of the strong spiritual foundation God wanted to lay down in my life. I had nothing else to focus on externally, as my life was not much to look at during this period, so I was forced to go inward and focus on building up my own heart with God through facing the darkness and fear and replacing it with peace.

Building a strong foundation meant that I had to go right down to the darkest and blackest core of my own heart to begin to build. I had to build from the parts of my life where the pain ran deepest. The various trials I encountered once I became a Christian helped to push me into this darkened place so that I could see and embrace the full extent of what was there. This was a very lonely and sometimes despairing process, one that I often did not feel comfortable sharing with other people, even Christians, as many of them did not understand what was happening to me.

Some of the greatest revelations that truly changed my life came out of a place of total fatigue and exhaustion. I actually found that being tired physically and mentally actually helped me get into a place where I could become more aware of what was happening within me and therefore become free of it. I learned that even though I felt over-emotional when I was tired, simply trying to rest or sleep was not always the answer, and I needed to look at what emotion the tiredness was revealing. If I wasn't in a place of fatigue, there was a good chance I could have overlooked it, as it may not have surfaced due to my emotional awareness being lower. I was one of those people who felt depressed and often irritable when over-tired. God used these situations to help me become more aware of what was truly happening within me. In a way, being tired actually did me a lot of good, as it helped me to bring the issues I needed to face to the surface rather than keeping them brewing below.

I received a lot of advice from well-meaning Christian people telling me that I needed to stop focusing on the negative and turn my mind back to positive things. Though I could understand why they were saying that, this was the exact opposite of what I really needed to do in order to build a strong foundation of strength and peace. If you are going to build a house on soft land, you simply cannot afford to just start building on a damp and unstable foundation. You have to dig into the depths of it and replace the muck with concrete so that your house will stand strong. The concrete will not dig its own hole and pour itself in there. Neither will the soft, unstable land jump out of the ground and make a place for you to build on. You have to fight to break through it.

The trials faced by Christians are sometimes brought upon them by their own actions and sometimes the works of others, but very often—from my experience—the source of the trial is God Himself. That is not to say that God initiates trials, but many of them are specifically allowed by Him so that we can learn something. I know that God has put me into some very black places over the years. Well-meaning people have come and done their best to try and get me out, but the honest reality of the situation was that God had put me in that dark place and wanted me to remain there until I learned what He had in mind for me to learn.

I believe strongly that if the church is to see a greater influx of people coming through its doors to know Christ, it needs to first build its own foundations to the point that it is strong enough to handle the harvest that God wants to bless it with. We need to learn not to despair of the barren places that God puts us into and instead learn to take from them what He wants us to learn. We must learn to let Him take us out of them when we are ready rather than trying to get out of them ourselves.

Every believer must face this on their own, as no one can be spiritually strong through the faith or spiritual strength of another person. It is not easy. It is lonely, isolating, and often discouraging, but this process must be embraced if a strong foundation is to be laid in the lives of believers and the church itself.

HOW IGNORANCE CAN RUIN THE PRESENT AND CONTAMINATE THE FUTURE

The ignorance I based my life around resulted in me trying to use people and circumstances to help me to ignore the truth about myself, as I thought that this would bring me some kind of happiness. One of my strongest desires when I was younger, especially throughout the early years of my faith, was to get married. I built marriage and intimacy up in my mind as the ultimate fix to all of my problems. I would spend day and night thinking about it and praying for my future wife and looked forward to the future when everything would be fixed because I was married. I became extremely frustrated when it did not happen for me and I saw it happening for others around me. I felt overlooked and even blamed God for this at times.

Eventually I began to realize why this was happening and why God seemed to be deliberately withholding something from me that I felt that I needed. I slowly began to realize that although finding the right person for marriage is important, what is just as important is becoming the right person yourself. While I was in that time of ignorance and praying constantly for a wife I was still strongly rooted in my old habits of ignorance, addiction, and the subsequent boredom which would eventually set in due to my refusal to deal with myself. God showed me that if I had married at that young age, while still very unhealed and confused, initially it would no doubt have been fantastic, but all it would have really done was suppress the darkness I carried within me for a short time. It would eventually come back up again. It would then translate through me blaming my wife for my own feelings and emotional and spiritual dissatisfaction, and leave me feeling both disgusted with her and with myself for marrying her in the first place. Marriage would have been unable to fix me like I expected that it would have.

I barricaded my own heart up to keep it safe in my mind, and I felt that I could get through a relationship by keeping the girl on the outside and using her to satisfy my needs without any need for a deeper connection. I did not feel I could cope with this, as I was strongly embedded in the mentality that I would be thrown out of people's lives—even people that claimed to love me—if I were to have an argument with them. God tried to impress upon me that marriage would bring about different problems and in many ways would actually make things harder for me (especially once the honeymoon period wore off) and that arguments and disagreements would happen, as they were part of an honest and healthy relationship. However, I simply blocked out what God was saying to me and went back into my own little fantasy world of how great everything would be once this happened for me and how I would live happily ever after in my little bubble of ignorance from the truth about marriage—and the truth about myself.

Due to my belief that people only appreciated me for what I could do for them to make them happy and my fear of putting people to the test when they said that they cared about me, I found it difficult to have honest and authentic relationships with people, especially when I found a girl that I liked. I felt very much as if I were putting on a show while I was around them to try and make myself look appealing rather than just sitting back and being real. I was terrified of being real, as I was afraid that people would not like what they saw and that all of a sudden I would not be making them happy anymore. So, I did the best I could to remain in a place of fakeness at all times. I was terrified of testing other people in regard to whether or not they really loved me, as that gave them power to either take me as I was or reject me. The simple solution in my own naivety was to never test anyone or anything and control circumstances so vigorously so that nothing bad could ever happen. This was not based in reality, and if I had entered a relationship with the expectation of being able to maintain this façade it would have been a catastrophe. These feelings were all connected to the stronghold of rejection I held in my life at the time.

I would have lost everything due to my own inflated expectations of marriage, and the destruction of these dreams, fueled by my own negligence, would have driven me into a blacker place of depression than ever before. This would have happened because everything that I was wishing for and dreaming of would not have been able to satisfy me, and I would have been stuck in a commitment that I didn't really want to be a part of anymore. That was because commitment wasn't what I really wanted; all I really wanted was release from my problems, which this situation was unable to give me. I sincerely doubt any marriage could have held this burden and probably would have broken up, leaving both me and my wife far worse than ever before. Because I refused to acknowledge or deal with my spiritual and emotional problems I would have been setting myself up for absolute destruction in the future.

Once the honeymoon period was over in my dealings with people (e.g., if I started a new job) after some time they would often appear to be more moody toward me, and I would feel that this was because they no longer liked me and wanted me gone. In reality, what I believe was actually happening was that they were now used to me and trusted me and treated me as "part of the furniture," so to speak, whereas due to my own unhealed emotions and wrong mind-sets I would interpret the situation differently. The situation would eventually end up with me leaving out of anger and bitterness, all the while looking ahead to greener pastures, not knowing that the pollutant that would inevitably destroy the pastures I was heading to actually came from within me. This line of thinking had me leave countless jobs and living situations over the years and no doubt would have destroyed a marriage, had I married young, as I had prayed for.

I think also that my negative and fearful mind-sets would have produced a controlling and belittling nature while in the home, which would have hurt my wife and undoubtedly my children if I were to have had any. Through refusing to deal with myself I would have passed on my negative attributes to them and continued the cycle. Fortunately, God was gracious enough to give me the chance to break these cycles and stop them at the source, which is something I cannot thank Him enough for, as I would not want my children to have to face what I have faced in my life.

Though I am still single, I look back and I thank God that He did not answer my prayers back then. Those prayers, were they to be answered, would have destroyed me and some poor, unsuspecting girl. I am grateful that God helped me to obtain what I truly needed, which was a way to turn my pain into strength, insight, and clarity. I began to realize that, for me, marriage and inti-mate relationships should not be looked upon as a place to strive toward in order to make everything OK but rather a place that I should be ready for once I am strong enough emotionally and spiritually to handle myself and the relationship adequately. Only after learning these lessons could I feel more ready for approaching a relationship.

I cannot help but wonder how many people out there have entered into relationships with others carrying this belief system within their hearts, only to end up bitterly disappointed and dissatisfied and heaping unnecessary pain on the other person for not being able to fix their problems. I believe that this shallow and selfish way of thinking has destroyed countless marriages and relationships over the years, and I truly thank God that I was able to avoid inevitably becoming one of these statistics, and for giving me the chance to get things right in the future and to base a relationship on the right foundation.

BREAKING OUT OF COMFORT ZONES

Before I began to learn how to heal, managing OCD in my life was all about creating and remaining within comfort zones. Managing the anxiety was all I knew how to do at the time, so it seemed like the best option. Most of my energy went into trying to create a safe environment for myself. Any time I felt as if my comfort zone was threatened, I would react badly until I felt I had regained some kind of control over the comfort zone so that I would feel safe again.

I remember once when I was very young I was in the car with my mother, and I asked her what would happen if she let go of the steering wheel. My honest thoughts at the time were that if she let the steering wheel go the car would run off crazily in a thousand different directions at once, trying to be absolutely everywhere at all times, because it had nothing guiding it or holding it back from going wherever it wanted. I was genuinely surprised when my mother told me that the car would probably just carry on in a straight line and perhaps drift off to the side a bit until she took hold of the wheel again.

Though this story is humorous, it is a good insight into what my mind was really like even back then. I honestly felt that if things were not perfectly planned and controlled—and therefore fully known—that they would just go completely crazy due to lack of guidance. I could not handle the concept of anything happening without my exclusive control and intervention, which meant I had to know everything about it in order to eliminate that fear of the unknown and not give it any room to move. It was as if I lived my life on a straight, fully lit path with pitch black areas on both sides. The black areas were unknown, so I kept to the safe, lit path, as it was the path that I knew and could predict exactly what was going to happen. Life was boring at best—but predictable.

I resented God for taking me out of my comfort zones to begin with, as I just wanted to feel safe, and I could not understand why God seemingly did not want this for me. Thankfully, I realized that life with God is all about going forward and that life should not be about simply managing everything and keeping everything controlled and safe till the end. It should be an adventure, one that takes the individual to the highest peaks and into the lowest valleys so that they can truly learn to appreciate and experience life to the fullest.

As I thought about this it made me realize what my life would have become if Christ had not gotten hold of me. I never would have done anything to challenge myself and never would have ventured out of my comfort zone. I would have built my whole life around ignorance and denial, only to realize once I got to the end of my life that I had missed countless opportunities that were given to me and that life had now passed me by. I could see myself coming to the end of my life with absolutely nothing to show for it except a useless existence spent trying to run from issues I had contained within myself.

I believe that deliberately choosing to remain within comfort zones is a contributing factor to depression and anxiety within western society. Think about it. If you have issues brewing deep within your mind, they will weigh upon and sap your quality of life, often without you even realizing it. If the human heart is never fully challenged and its core foundations are not shaken, then the issues within can never be truly confronted, and they just remain in darkness. Though the person in question can have everything that they have ever wanted in their lives as well as every dream fulfilled, they will mean nothing to a heart that is not fully able to appreciate them due to leaving issues in darkness.

I believe that God wishes to take all believers on this journey of life where they must learn not to rely on their own exclusive need for control but learn to be able to trust in God's judgment and coordination of their lives and circumstances. This is especially difficult for those who have struggled with anxiety and depression such as myself. These strongholds can appear incredibly daunting and can feel indestructible. However, God freely grants wisdom and insight to those who ask for it and is more than prepared to do His part in helping us to become a truly free people. The only question is, Are we prepared to do our part?

THE DANGER OF POWER

"Power corrupts, and absolute power corrupts absolutely"—a famous quote from Lord Acton in 1887. I believe this statement to be very true, although my interpretation of it is slightly different. I believe power simply reveals what is already within our own hearts and gives us a choice as to how we act on what is inside of us.

How often in life do we see power abused by those who use power the wrong way for their own personal gain? All of us throughout our lives are given power, and I believe God watches how we use it. When we walk into a store and ask the store person for something we are in a position of power since the person behind the counter is being paid to serve us. We can use that power to make their day a little bit easier by being polite and pleasant, even if we have a problem, and by being respectful. Parents have power too. Children are strongly influenced by their parents' behavior toward them. In many ways, especially at younger ages, the future of the child is in the hands of the parent. Managers have power over their staff. They can choose how they treat those they employ.

I believe one of the true tests of character is how to

handle power. The true danger with power is that it is an easy avenue for corruption, as for a person within power it is very easy for the person in question to abuse the power that is given to them, and very often, they are able to get away with it. My honest belief with power is that power can give room for the fullness of self-expression, and often in positions of power people express themselves out of parts of themselves that they do not know or understand. It is like a person who is characterized as being weak and fearful but all of a sudden gains some kind of power and creates a reign of terror, which they are now free to do without fear of consequence. All of that hurt and negative emotion translates in a different way and becomes a powerful fuel for tyranny and domination. The dark places in that person's life are given room to flow freely through their actions, which are unchecked due to the power that has been given to them.

One of the main characteristics of God is that He never places someone into a position He does not believe that they are ready for. For example, the story of Joseph in the Bible is a prime example of this. The young man has dreams of rulership and enthusiastically tells his brothers and family about the dream he has. His brothers respond by casting him into a pit and selling him as a slave to the Egyptians. Joseph spends years in prison and is falsely accused of many things throughout this time, including being accused of sleeping with Potiphar's wife.

However, he does his time and eventually is promoted

into a glorious position of power—being second in charge of the entire kingdom of Egypt, second only to the pharaoh himself. Joseph then meets with his brothers who cast him into the pit years earlier, yet times have changed. They do not recognize him, as they have not seen him for years, and come to him begging for food. Joseph could have refused and thrown his brothers out, or even chosen to have them tortured or killed, and it would be easy to understand why. However, Joseph chooses not to abuse his power and blesses his brothers.

I believe that Joseph was forced to come face to face with the full extent of who he really was while he was in jail. It would have been so easy for him to remain angry and bitter and understandably feel very justified in doing so, as, after all, he had done nothing to deserve being in prison and certainly did not deserve to be accused of sleeping with Potiphar's wife. However, my belief is that Joseph was firmly placed in that prison—by God Himself—so that he would have to come face to face with the full extent of himself and would be able to thoroughly search and examine his own heart with no external distractions to sway him from his task.

This may be easily looked upon as a bitter and unfair thing that was dealt to Joseph by the hand of God. However, in reality, it was anything but, as God was using the immense injustice heaped upon Joseph to prepare him for leadership and used his time of imprisonment as a time for Joseph to thoroughly get to know God—and himself. He had to take a stark, brutally honest look at himself and was forced to either deal with what was inside him and learn from it or sit and suffer in his misery. Joseph took the necessary way out of the situation, and God blessed him for it.

My belief is that, had Joseph not responded in this way to the hand that was dealt to him, God would never have promoted him to the position he found himself in, as the immense power that was given to him would have shown up every single character flaw in his entire life and heart. He would have been free to exploit the power for his own gain and impress his character flaws on others as he saw fit. If Joseph was in this position of power and had not dealt with his own heart, he could easily have decided to kill his brothers in order to take revenge for their mistreatment of him years earlier—and no doubt could have found a justifiable reason to do so if challenged. However, because Joseph was a man of character, a quality forged into him during his time in prison, he chose to take the right path and defer any judgment on his brothers to the hands of God, who is the only just and true Judge.

I believe Joseph also knew that even though he was only accountable to one man in Egypt, the pharaoh himself, he was accountable for the way he used his power to God, and he knew that God was holding him responsible for the use of the power that was given to him. If he had chosen to abuse the power that was given to him he may have been able to get away with it throughout his lifetime. However, at the end of his life he would have had to answer to God Himself.

The perfect example of power that is not misused is

found in God. He has the power to create and destroy equally easily. Jesus said when He was going to the cross that He could have had twelve legions of angels at His side at a moment's notice if He asked for them. (See Matthew 26:53.) However, He chose not to and chose instead to face the fate given to Him by His Father. God could have chosen to destroy us the moment we sinned against Him and could have chosen to wipe the human race off the face of the earth—yet He chose not to.

ANGER—NOT ALWAYS A BAD THING

We have already looked at the danger of misguided anger. However, there is another side to this story as well. There are times when we are called as Christians, especially Christian men, to stand up and fight. I believed that all anger was wrong and that anger was to be avoided at all times. I used to feel a strong sense of self-hatred whenever I found myself in a position of truly feeling and expressing anger. Although this teaching had some basis of truth in it—uncontrolled and unchecked anger can be sinful and create further sin—this is not the whole truth, as there is another side to the story.

Jesus offended people, yet there was no sin in Him. When He went to the temple and threw out the people who were selling various things in the temple, no doubt He would have copped a lot of criticism for what He did. I can just imagine people saying, "How could the supposed Son of God act like that? What an irrational response." However, Jesus was confident and strong enough within Himself and what He believed in to know that He had a right to be angry and that He needed to make no apologies for what He did. He was not concerned if people were offended by what He did, as He knew that He did the right thing in the eyes of God.

So many portrayals of Jesus almost try to present Him as feminine, which is understandable in a way, as God calls Himself the God of peace. However, I do not believe these portrayals are accurate. Jesus was a carpenter before He came into His ministry. I've worked on the odd building site over the years, and from my experience, carpenters tend to be fairly tough characters. Jesus was no hippy. Though He did proclaim peace, He also recognized that there was a time and a place for anger. God does not say, "Don't get angry." He says in the Book of Ephesians 4:26: "In your anger do not sin. Do not let the sun go down while you are still angry." This is the real challenge—learning to respond adequately to situations with anger when necessary, yet to keep anger righteous and not use it as a vehicle to express other emotions. It also calls us to resolve our anger on the spot, at the time of the situation, rather than to bottle it up and let it fester, something I have been very guilty of doing over the years.

It can be far too easy to judge people when it comes to anger. I found from my own journey that there were times when others had every right to be angry with me. However, I would feel offended at their anger, and I could spread that offence around if I chose to. My offence—and my subsequent choosing to spread the offence to others via gossip—was actually my problem, not theirs at all. Those who are able to embrace anger with a clear head and use it properly are using anger the way that it is meant to be used, in my opinion. The challenge is learning to differentiate between anger that comes from a place of clear thinking and anger that comes from a place of emotional confusion seeking an outlet. I believe the latter sort of anger is not right, because emotional confusion and frustration that seeks an outlet is never really solved through hostile confrontation. It will only add to the cycle of injustice, especially if the person on the receiving end is in a similar emotional state of mind. In that state, even if the situation in question is seemingly resolved, I believe the anger is just bottled up.

I believe anger gets a bad rap in the modern-day world, especially in Christian circles. My honest belief is that many Christians have bottled up and ignored their own anger, as they somehow felt that it was not appropriate or "Christian" to be seen as being angry. When faced with situations where other Christians act with anger for whatever reason, they can very quickly jump out and condemn them for showing anger and tell them that it is not Christlike, even though the person in question may have every right to be angry and may be doing it with a clear head.

I believe the tools to think with and the techniques outlined in this book can truly help people to learn to embrace anger in a far healthier and less destructive way. They embrace it in a way that is actually seeking a solution, rather than a way that is just seeking a release that will never come.

My own approach to anger and confrontation has hugely benefited from these techniques, and I am able to embrace seemingly volatile situations in a far better and far healthier manner than before. With each little bit I deal with, the stronger my peace gets; and the stronger my peace gets, the better I cope with what I am faced with.

MEEKNESS VERSUS WEAKNESS

This has always been a very interesting topic for me. Being a very fearful person, with fears that have continued to be revealed and dealt with throughout my Christian walk, my behavior would often come across as being meek and mild, kind and gentle; however, internally it was the absolute opposite. The concept of meekness as mentioned in the Bible was deeply offensive to me, as I loathed my fearful behavior and wanted to break out of it, yet I felt as if I was being instructed by the Bible that being weak and spineless and full of fear was how I was meant to be.

I believe people who have struggled with bullying and the pain and frustration that goes along with this are very often deeply frustrated with the concept of meekness and "turning the other cheek." It very much seemed to me that I was simply allowing myself to face further abuse and that I was allowing my self-esteem and self-respect to be destroyed even further, which made this teaching a very hard pill to swallow. It made me feel as if God was a wimp and that He was asking me to be a wimp as well, which made me feel angry and also made me want to rebel against what I believed God was like. Fortunately, through years of God-inspired soul-searching and analysis of my own heart and mind, I began to learn the truth about this issue.

My journey in this area was somewhat different to many others. Facing my fears helped me to free my own anger and become more comfortable with expressing it. God was helping me to learn to feel my own strength and power so that I would slowly begin to learn that I was not as weak as I once believed. I had always looked at myself in the mirror and seen a very weak person staring back at me. Even though others would tell me that I was strong, I never for a moment believed them. Once God helped me start to strip away the fears and insecurities that kept my fury and other emotions trapped within me, this perception of self-weakness began to change, and I began to truly believe that I was a strong person after all.

As I learned to feel my own strength and power, I began to realize that there were often times when I was faced with a situation that I knew I was able to stand up to and fight against if I wanted to. However, instead of backing down out of fear or charging in with aggression, I felt a peace about simply sitting back and letting things unfold. It was like God took me to a place where I learned to truly feel my own strength so that I would know that I was capable of fighting when I needed to, but then He took me to a place of learning to be responsible with the newfound strength that had been forged into me. I learned a fundamental truth: just because you can do something, doesn't always mean that you should.

Throughout this journey I learned the vital difference between meekness and weakness. Weakness for me involved submitting to fear that still ruled over unseen parts of my life, which was never something God wanted for me. Meekness involved knowing that I had the capability to do something about a certain situation if I wanted to yet choosing not to.

There is a huge difference between true, tested emotional strength and the macho behavior we see out in the world today. True strength comes from a place of peace and a clear head. Macho posing is simply an exercise in trying to stifle something within oneself. When people try to convince others through their actions that they are strong, they are setting themselves up for destruction, as everything is based on trying to stifle one's fears, and that will eventually collapse. People can distance themselves so much through trying to run from their own feelings using macho behavior that they can forget who they really are. There is nothing strong about forcing your fears back within yourself and trying to convince everybody that they do not exist, including yourself. This is nothing but an exercise in frustration and exhaustion.

Men who are truly strong are those who are able to learn to face up to their own weaknesses and turn pain into peace. They are not driven to react by unhealed emotions when faced with a testing situation but are able to respond in a place of meekness and rational thinking with the self-assurance and focused mind to be able to act assertively if needed. This is true strength, and the type of strength God wants His people to have.

Learning the difference between meekness and weakness and actually putting it into practice was never going to be a quick fix for me. I very often still face issues in my life that I respond to out of fear and weakness rather than meekness. It is not a destination but a process, one that goes deeper and deeper into my emotions and fully exposes each fear that is found there. However, as I have continued to journey through my fears and deal with them I have begun to realize that there are many situations that I now respond to with strength, either outwardly or inwardly, through meekness, where I used to respond with fear. Even though it can often feel like I am going round in circles, I am able to look back on my life and realize that I have made progress in this area.

Effectiveness of the Modern-day Church

Much has been made of the modern-day church and Christianity in western society. Some Christian figures in the public light have been shown up for leading double lives—one life of supposed holiness, which they present to the world, and another hidden life of sin, which has inevitably brought a lot of accusations onto the church itself.

I believe that if the church is to see a greater influx of people coming through its doors and getting saved, the church needs to get itself right and strengthen the core of its own foundations with God. Only then will it be able to handle the greater influx of unsaved people coming to know the Lord and the responsibility and pressure that it will inevitably bring.

It is too easy in the modern-day world—even for Christians—to become swept up in a life of distractions. It is very easy to pretend to be a Christian in the world today. You can pepper conversations with so-called spiritual talk, lift your hands and close your eyes during songs, and attend every Christian conference and event possible.

Of course, there is nothing wrong with any of these things. However, without a true, honest, warts-and-all relationship with God, none of these things truly count for anything. My opinion is that the church is stagnating in many ways because people are becoming stuck in their personal and spiritual lives. This is often because they lack the wisdom and the reflection to be able to honestly take stock of where their lives are at. The Bible says, "My people are destroyed from lack of knowledge" (Hosea 4:6). My belief regarding this scripture is that God's people are destroyed by a lack of knowledge about themselves and a lack of knowledge regarding how to truly break through the darkness and turn it into light.

It is too easy for people to hide in church and get by with superficial, shallow relationships with those around them. If the issues in the lives of Christians are brought out into the open and darkness is turned into light and wisdom, it can be used to greatly benefit those around us and help them to break free as well. We need honesty—with God, with others, and with ourselves.

Treating others with kindness and adopting a meek response to anger are all well and good, provided that they come out of a genuinely changed heart. If they are responses out of fear, those around you will be able to sense this and may well feel that Christianity is a crutch for the fearful and weak minded. I believe that God does want His people to respond in a kind-hearted manner, but not from a place of fear. People can spot a fake a mile off. It is this sort of thing that breeds the attitude of disgust toward the church, as people will see someone who appears to be good and kind until something happens that pushes them into a dark place and they aren't able to cope with it. Others will then get the idea that they were faking it all along.

Of course, there is another side to this. That person may well have been acting in as genuine a manner, as they were capable of until something happened to them to push them into an emotional zone that they felt uncomfortable with. That does happen, as God uses difficulties to further refine and grow His people. This is why I believe we should put it across to others that Christians still struggle a lot as well, so that they will not expect to see perfection in the church but in God Himself. What they should expect to see in the church are those who are on the path of learning to become whole in Christ and are walking honestly with themselves and with others.

Simply going to church on a Sunday is not going to change anything. Our entire lives need to be based around what we believe in, and our lives need to be a showpiece as to what we believe in. We need to be seen as people who are continually changing for the better and are not afraid of honesty. We cannot sit around and expect other people to be better Christians. We need to start doing it ourselves. I came up with this little quote a few years back, which has helped me greatly along my journey:

> Do not expect people and circumstances to change without doing anything yourself—begin to change yourself, and you will see change begin to happen around you.

I believe this is also how the church needs to function as a whole. We can't sit around and expect others to repent or to forgive us or to reach out more or to have better attitudes. That is really up to them. We can advise them, of course, but we need to get our own heart right with God first and be committed to continually changing for the better in our own lives.

I also believe that more time and effort needs to go toward helping new Christians—especially young people—in their journeys. I was very fortunate to have a caring and understanding spiritual mentor in my mother when I rededicated my life to Christ. If I had not had this mentoring I do not know how long I would have lasted.

The Holy Spirit started raising up the deeply entrenched issues in my heart not long after I rededicated my life to Christ. I could not understand what was happening to me in this regard, and very often God would cop the blame for "making me feel bad." It would have been very easy for me to have looked to the world I had come from and said that this was easier to go back to, as I now felt worse than ever. Of course, this was never going to be a solution, but I did not understand this at the time and could easily have slipped back if I wanted to.

It took a long time and a lot of counseling and prayer from caring Christian mentors before I started to develop the realization that true peace and joy came through going through issues rather than avoiding them. I still needed to find my answers from God and God alone regarding the deepest areas of pain that I could not define myself, as I could not rely solely on others to help me through, since I knew that I could burn them out if I were not careful. It was only through constant encouragement from God and others that I was able to develop this ability and to realize that God was actually using all of this to help me become a stronger person.

I realized just how easy it was for people to become bitter and discouraged at Christianity and fall away from the faith. I have seen it happen, especially those with deeply rooted issues in their lives, such as myself. They just feel so awful that they think that they are better off where they were and therefore fall away from the faith due to lack of knowledge and understanding of how

God changes people. As a result they cut themselves off from what they truly need the most.

The Importance of Grace

The Bible speaks of God as being a God of grace and mercy as well as a God of justice. My journey to discovering grace was a gradual one. There was never any true grace or mercy in my heart before I became a Christian, only a façade of grace and humility which was based in fear, not in love at all and therefore not genuine. It was hard for me to see God as gracious due to my own issues, which clouded my ability to perceive God in an accurate light. Therefore, seeing as I struggled to see God as gracious, it made it very difficult for me to extend grace to others.

Learning about the grace of God did not happen for me overnight. I knew about it in my head, but knowing about it in my heart and emotions was a totally different story. It took many years of prayer and introspection before I was able to truly begin to perceive and understand the grace of God and how much He has chosen to suffer on our behalf in the name of love.

One of the most influential figures in my life in this regard was my mother. When I was experiencing some of my darkest days in my mid-teenage years I often came across as hostile, moody, and anti-social. It could have been very easy for many people around me to write me off as a total no-hoper, and in many ways they would have been quite accurate in their judgment. However, my mother, a strong Christian, stood by me and supported me no matter what. I also saw radical change for the better in her life, which was one of the strongest influences that helped me on the way to recommitting my life to Christ. She could easily have judged me for my actions and given up on me, but she chose not to, and in the end her love and grace despite my hostility helped me turn my life around for the better.

She showed me that God was gracious to me and loved me despite my shortcomings. Not to say for a second that she would tolerate behavior that could put her or anyone else in any kind of danger, as that is by no means wise, but God would stick by me and help me through it. Due to my mental health issues and emotional struggles I often felt very alienated from the world around me as a child, especially at school. This made it very easy for me to slip into a mind-set that said, "Everyone and everything hates me, so I hate everything and everyone in return." Seeing this kind of loving treatment from my mother truly helped me to realize that there was something different about her, and that thing was Christ.

I realize now that we would be nothing without the grace of God and that many people will only come to know Christ through seeing true godly grace extended to them by believers—even when they do not deserve it. There is definitely a lack of this to some degree in the church. Throughout my Christian walk I myself have had times when I felt unable to control my emotions due to overwhelming personal circumstances. This was coupled with the frustration of not yet being able to identify the true source of the pain I was feeling in order to free myself of it. Admittedly I was out of line, but people who claimed to call themselves Christians would often judge and reject me due to my actions and sometimes even call my faith into question as a result. Though they could justify their judgment due to my actions, which were often out of line, the question must be asked, Would Christ have done the same thing?

Think about it: how often in Scripture does Jesus show compassion to those around Him, even those deeply immersed in sin? The story of the prostitute is always one that warms my heart.

> But Jesus went to the Mount of Olives. At dawn he appeared again in the temple courts, where all the people gathered around him, and he sat down to teach them. The teachers of the law and the Pharisees brought in a woman caught in adultery. They made her stand before the group and said to Jesus, "Teacher, this woman was caught in the act of adultery. In the Law Moses commanded us to stone such women. Now what do you say?" They were using this question as a trap, in order to have a basis for accusing him. But Jesus bent down and started to write on the ground with his finger. When they kept on questioning him, he straightened up and said to them, "If any one of you is without sin, let him be the first to throw a stone at her." Again he stooped down and wrote on the ground. At this, those who heard began

to go away one at a time, the older ones first, until only Jesus was left, with the woman still standing there. Jesus straightened up and asked her, "Woman, where are they? Has no one condemned you?" "No one, sir," she said. "Then neither do I condemn you," Jesus declared. "Go now and leave your life of sin."

—JOHN 8:1–11

Christ did not condemn this woman's actions; however, He did not condone them either. It is this sort of grace and compassion, even for those who are in the wrong, which will truly save people and bring people closer to God. I have struggled to receive the grace of God in the past due to the emotional and spiritual strongholds I have battled with that have kept me in a legalistic frame of mind, saying that I will be condemned if I do anything wrong. It is far easier for me to become defensive in the face of another person's perceived hostility or supposed sinfulness than it is for me to try and understand where they are coming from and extend grace to them as a result. But my heart is changing for the better slowly but surely as I learn to receive the grace of God. I believe it must first be received before it can be truly given out.

THE JOURNEY CONTINUES

I am very pleased to say I have much more peace in my life now, and my circumstances have hugely improved recently. I am able to face situations with more confidence and strength than ever before. I sleep far better at night, I have more energy during the day, and my overall enjoyment of life has increased hugely. People who have known me best over the years have noticed a huge change in me. I have far more freedom in my life now. My life has gone from a turbulent shambles of instability, shattered hope, and forced obedience to fearful emotions to actually being able to make my own decisions and achieve things I would never have attempted unless I had been on this journey. The Bible says this, which has become so relevant to me, "So if the Son sets you free, you will be free indeed" (John 8:36).

Despite the enormous distance that I have come, the journey is by no means over for me. I am still journeying through these things, although the hard times are not nearly as frequent now as what they used to be. I have learned how to handle them the way that God wants me to. I am now beginning to feel as if so much of my life that I felt was so senseless and so awful in so many ways is finally beginning to make sense. I am reminded of the following scripture, "'Neither this man nor his parents sinned,' said Jesus, 'but this happened so that the work of God might be displayed in his life'" (John 9:3). Of course, I cannot say that I have not sinned, as I know that I have sinned greatly throughout my lifetime. However, my hope is that the glory of God will be able to be displayed in my life through what I have become—and what I am still in the process of becoming.

I do not know what would have become of me, had God not gotten hold of me and helped me to learn to change. I could easily have led a life controlled by violence and abuse due to the overpowering destructive desires I had within my own heart. I could also have gone the other way and turned my destructive tendencies upon myself and taken my own life. Either way, I would be very surprised if I would have lived as long as I have. I am thankful that God gave me the chance to overcome everything that has plagued me. Without His continual guidance and endless patience with me I never would have come to the place I am coming into now.

People may believe that Christianity is for weak, spineless people who need a crutch to help them get through life. My experience of Christianity has taught me that God wants to take everyone—especially those who are deeply flawed and broken, such as myself—and turn their brokenness into true and tested strength and clarity. It is by no means easy. Warming a pew in church is easy. Truly following God is one of the hardest things to do, but it is the only path to true peace.

This journey has also taught me the horrifying reality of abortion and what it does to human beings. Ever since I realized that the fear of being aborted was the main cause of my mental sickness I have been developing a huge heart for unborn children. In a way, due to the fear I inherited, I know what it's like to face the horror of facing abortion in the womb, which basically becomes like a coffin. My heart is deeply grieved for the massacre of these living human beings and the unbearable terror that tears their souls and bodies to shreds.

We also have a real enemy out there in Satan. He truly hates all people, not just Christians, and will stop at nothing to destroy them. He uses every bit of darkness he can to try and hide the rotten truth about who he is and will use circumstances to try to get people to destroy each other rather than face the truth. He wants people to abuse and destroy each other. He has no respect for anyone and will stop at nothing to destroy anyone he can through ignorance and deception. I am grateful that God has given me the chance to identify his dark and insidious methods of controlling and deceiving people and break through them, as well as the ability to write and hopefully share some of this insight with others.

Though the subject matter of this book is by its nature fairly dark, it is ultimately a story of victory and hope. My story is proof that even some of the deepest and most complicated psychological issues can be overcome through prayer and guidance from God, coupled with determination and courage. I know for a fact that my mental health has improved thanks to utilizing the tools to think with that I have outlined in this book. When something happens that previously would have caused a sense of overwhelming negative emotion, now it does not affect me at all. It is a slow process—but a necessary one.

My hope is that those who are reading this book may be able to see something in what I have written that they can identify with in their own lives and subsequently realize that they are not alone in the world—and that there is a way out for them. If I can do that, then the book will have been worthwhile. In my journey I have met a great God; my prayer is that you do too.

ABOUT THE AUTHOR

GRAHAM AITCHISON IS twenty-eight years old and has held a strong Christian faith for the past eleven years. He was deeply unstable before he became a Christian, and throughout his journey of faith he went through many deep valleys which forced him to come face to face with the darkest aspects of his own heart. This journey has included long periods of unemployment, severe physical sickness, and numerous failures both regarding personal relationships and employment. Throughout all of these experiences he has grown immensely. These experiences have helped him develop wisdom and an insight into mental illness and how to grow as a Christian. He has preached to congregations on many different occasions.

CONTACT THE AUTHOR

Facebook:
www.facebook.com/GrahamIanAitchison

Twitter:
https://twitter.com/GrahamAitchison

Blog:
http://giaitchison.blogspot.co.nz/